The Authors

Tracie O'Keefe is a practising hypnotherapist, psychotherapist and counsellor with a degree in Clinical Hypnotherapy. She practises both at the London Medical Centre in Harley Street as well as running her own private practice in Regent Street. She constantly deals with many transsexuals, who attend her clinic and is presently on the doctorate programme with the American Institute of Hypnotherapy. Herself a transsexual, she sought many years ago to become her own concept of womanhood, only years later to find that the lure of lesbian love led her in a direction far beyond her wildest dreams.

After completing a degree in Performance Arts at Middlesex Polytechnic, Katrina Fox wrote as the Camp Vamp, glamorous gossip columnist in one of London's gay magazines, "OUT". She currently works as an actress, model and is studying linguistics at the University of Westminster.

This book is dedicated to all those lovers, friends,
families and professionals who have helped and
continue to help transsexuals along their way.

TRANS-✖-U-ALL
The Naked Difference

BY TRACIE O'KEEFE and KATRINA FOX

Published by:
Extraordinary People Press
Suite 412 Triumph House
185 – 191 Regent Street
London W1R 7WB
Tel. 0171 734 3749
Fax. 0171 439 3536
E-Mail katfox@easynet.co.uk
Web site http://easyweb.easynet.co.uk/~katfox/

First published 1997

British Library Cataloguing-in-Publication Data
A catalogue record for this book is available from the
British Library.

ISBN 0-9529482-0-6

Typeset by Elite Typesetting, Eastleigh, Great Britain

Printed by Antony Rowe Ltd, Chippenham, Great Britain

Distributed in the United Kingdom by Turnaround
Distribution

"It is the theory which decides what can be observed".
Einstein

"Why can't you teach a monkey to sing?"
"Because they don't speak Italian"
"Let me introduce you to Luigi Chimpanzee"
T.F. O'Keefe

In presenting this book we are attempting to show some of the differences in life.

There will be many other differences and we respect their right to exist and define themselves in accordance with their wishes.

Nothing is static, nothing is correct and nothing is true. . .

Contents

Acknowledgements   xii

Foreword   xiii

Preface   xv

Definitions and Redefinitions   xix

Tracie O'Keefe's Story   xxiii

CHAPTER ONE – THE PANSEXUAL THEORY
Introduction   1
The Pansexual Chart   5
Mascusexuals   6
Femisexuals   9

CHAPTER TWO – THE POSSIBLE CAUSES OF TRANSSEXUALISM
Stereotypes   12
Environmental influences   14
Social effects   16
Mascusexuals in the old Czechoslovakia   16
The third sex   17
Schizophrenia   17
It's all in the mind   18
Whose world is it anyway?   18
NLP   19
Body concepts   20
A mad compulsion?   21
Mothers to blame   22
Physical effects   23
Brainwaves   24
Brain composure   24
Re-incarnation   25
Hormonal imbalances   26
Hormones in the womb   27

Abnormalities in pregnancy   27
General Adaptation Theory   28
Chromosomal differentials   28
Genetics   29

CHAPTER THREE – DIAGNOSIS

Chromosome sexing   34
The SRY Gene   36
Psychiatry   37
Misdiagnosis   39
Expected gender roles   40
The life test   41
The rejection factor   42
Bad diagnoses by bad clinicians   44
The incidence of child abuse in the transsexual
    population   45
Disassociative disorders   45
The narcissistic factor   46
Diagnostic criteria   47

CHAPTER FOUR – TREATMENT

Hormonal treatment   48
Femisexuality and hormones   51
Mascusexuality and hormones   53

Surgery   55
Rhinoplasty   57
Ears   58
Facial implants   58
Jaw lines   58
Chin reduction   58
Lengthening of lower limbs   58
Frontal cranial reduction   59
Tracheal shave surgery   59
Surgery for raising the vocal pitch   59
Facelifts and eye jobs   60
Rib removal   60

Breast Augmentation   60
– Free floating silicone   61

– Through the nipple	62
– Under the arm	62
– Under the breast	62
– Capsular contraction	63
– The shape of things to come	63
Liposuction	64
Fat transfer	64
Collagen	64
Dermabrasion	64
Acid skin peel	65
Laser treatment	65
Laser tattoo removal	65
Mastectomy	65
Phalloplasty	66
Metaidoioplasty	69
Scrotoplasty	69
Urethroplasty	70
Orchidectomy	70
Vaginoplasty – Labia and Clitoplasty	70
Colonoplasty	73
Complications	73
Dilation	74
Costing	75
Transsexuality and HIV infection	76
Other treatments	**77**
Voice training	77
Behaviour Training Schools	77
Depilation	77
Counselling	78
Mind manipulation	79
Hypnotherapy	80
Pamela – a case history	83
Complisexual management	87
Rebuilding bigger, better, trannies	89

CHAPTER FIVE – LIVING AS A TRANSSEXUAL

Public transsexuals   91
The Julia Grant story   92
The importance of social networks   93
Mermaids   95
Small magazines and leaflets   95
Careers   95
Relationships   97
Childlessness   98
Children   99
Prostitution and transsexuality   100
Transsexuals in prison   101

CHAPTER SIX – POLITICS AND THE LAW

April Ashley   105
The medical profession   106
Toilets   106
Insurance   106
Portugal   107
Spain   107
Australia, New Zealand, Egypt and Turkey   107
Children and the law   107
Equality in England?   108
Private Members Bill for the rights of transsexuals   109
Conservative trannies   110
Marriage   110
A right to work   111
Cornwall County Council   112
Forming transsexual spaces   112
Time for change   113
Transsexuality, homosexuality, and transgenderism   114
Religion   116
Transsexualism and feminism   119
Lesbians and transsexuals   123
Transsexualism: The current medical viewpoint   125

Groups and organisations 126
International Conference on Transgendered Law &
   Employment Policy 126
Press for Change 126
Harry Benjamin International Gender Dysphoria
   Association Inc. 126

CHAPTER SEVEN – PERSONAL STORIES
Transsexual stories 128
Partners, friends and relatives 155

AFTERWORD 170

Appendix A – Trans-Diversity 172
Appendix B – Groups and organisations 176
Appendix C – Conferences 180

Bibliography 185
Papers 189
Videography 191
Films 192

Further Reading 193
Magazines 193
Books 194

Professional Resources 196

Internet and World Wide Web resources 197

Paper by Tracie O'Keefe 198

Call for comments 203

Index 204

Order form 208

Acknowledgements

We would like to thank all those who helped in the making of the book – especially to everyone who contributed their stories, experiences and photographs and to our friends and family for their support.

Special thanks also to:

Robin Lovell-Badge of the Medical Research Council for all his invaluable help with regard to the genetic information contained here.

Bernard Broughton of the Cell Mutation Unit at the University of Sussex for all his help with providing us with medical information and papers.

Penny Tyndale-Hardy of Mark Paterson and Associates for all her help and advice.

Foreword

Tracie O'Keefe and Katrina Fox have done a wonderful job lifting the veil on transsexuality. For the last forty five years I have had to listen to and be examined by the so-called experts, not least by Dr Valiant, Dr Randell, Professor Dewhurst, Professor Dent and others. What I think and would have to say about the above is unprintable so reading this book was like a breath of fresh air. I think that like the common cold transsexuality will always be a mystery, but I like to go along with the theory put forward by that marvellous man Dr. Nat Armstrong and that is that it all begins in the womb. However here is the first book that we the lay folk can understand.

You will meet extraordinary people living ordinary lives and *vice versa* in this book. All the most successful transsexuals that I have met and known are the ones whose lives were not destroyed by a sensationalist press. Mine was and I paid a heavy price for that. But that's another story. I know transsexuals who are doctors, surgeons, nurses, care-givers, shop assistants etc, in fact people across the whole spectrum of life and that is my point, they are just that – people, wonderful people most of them. They do very well but live with the threat that at any moment their lives could be shattered as mine was.

That is why I say it is time that the law caught up with medical science. Transsexuals are notoriously gentle people, usually with a great sense of humour (boy do they need it!), so why would Great Britain who preaches human rights to the rest of the world deny its own citizens their human rights? After all you are either for human rights or not – period. Transsexuals suffer enough on their isolated path to fulfilment, so why as we rush into the 21st century cannot one of the world's most sophisticated societies give up its hypocrisy on such a small section of society by giving them their full human rights? Allow them to change or at least alter their birth certificates, after all there is no going back for them and also allow them the pleasure and comfort of marriage without the threat of blackmail or worse. This is not a great deal to ask for.

More than three quarters of my life has been spent as a woman. I have never for one moment regretted my decision. I'm nice and kind to both people and animals and have worked very hard for years to improve our environment. Unfortunately I have had to spend most of my life abroad. It would be nice now as I go into my sixties to be able to come home to my beloved England as a full citizen. I urge you to read this book as it will give you some idea of what I'm talking about.

April Ashley

Preface

For most, sex is the final frontier. However, here are stories of people who span the sexes. It has been a popular misconception that transsexuals "change" their sex, when in fact they are born in no-man's-land and are faced with a battle to claim their believed identities. We, the authors, go far beyond any stereotypes, being one bisexual transsexual clinician practising in Harley Street, and the other, her glamorous actress/model lesbian lover.

Guaranteed to change your mind about those whom you thought changed their sex, this book will give you a window into the fascinating world of the sexual shape-shifters. Not written by a stuffy, reclusive academic, but by two people who live and experience transsexualism every day of their lives.

Here are the lifestyles, treatment and surgery of these desperate individuals who seek what they believe to be their real identities. You, the neighbour, friend or employer of these people often live alongside them, not knowing their terrifying fear of exposure. As many societies move towards accepting, supporting and incorporating transsexuals, still many cultures are conducting witch-hunts and denying these people passports, birth certificates, driving licences, insurance, the right to get married and even the right to vote under their chosen identity.

The development in medicine over the past sixty years, allowing transsexuals to undergo sex re-affirmation and gender reassignment therapy, has come as somewhat of a shock to society in general. Its apparent threatening demolition of the very roots of heterosexual family values has caused a paranoia about the subject. In a world of over rigid patriarchal cultures, some societies are unsure how to deal with what may appear to be the vulnerabilities within themselves. Much pain and anguish can accompany a life of transsexualism, inflicted on the whole by those who adopt a position of sexual elitism.

Medical assistance now afforded to transsexuals is driven by profit as much as anything else. The treatments can cost well up in excess of £100,000 and some get-rich-quick doctors are taking the money and performing sub-standard, life threatening surgeries. The patient, in some cases, after managing to get treatment, dies from it.

There is much talk and suggestion about the move towards holistic medicine. However, until the patriarchal male and female psycho-theorists begin to drop their authoritarian attitudes and respect the client's right to exist in any form, then they are unlikely to fulfil their Hippocratic promises. It is hard enough for those who consider themselves physically deformed to gain self respect, without alienation or patronisation from the very people they seek to help them. At this point it is important to tell you, the reader, that during the research of this book, we have met some clinicians with amazingly compassionate insight and we only hope that their example will be a model for others.

The emergence of transsexualism will not be going away and humankind throughout the world will have to find compromises in order to integrate these individuals into the mainstream. There is no humane reason why transsexuals should be denied the legal and social rights given automatically to everyone else. They are, after all, born a member of the human race and not, contrary to popular belief, made in Casablanca. There has, in recent times, been a series of biographies or autobiographies depicting the lives and experiences of transsexuals, some of the subjects having high public profiles. As yet society has failed to grasp the concept that transsexuality occurs throughout humanity and is not restricted to the notorious and nefarious. To the outsider it is a reality that initially appears to be an impossibility, but as science progresses, we explore how geneticists may one day reveal the root causes of such compelling behaviour.

Within these pages is a wide and varied explanation of all the relevant issues concerning these people who elude the strict male and female existence. As many transsexuals now begin to come out of the closet, we tell their stories of heartrending suffering and triumph over their condition. Alongside these, their relatives, friends, and lovers tell us how their lives have been affected too. We felt that the inclusion of such stories would be an invaluable and important contribution to the book, providing a broad spectrum of opinions and experiences on the subject of transsexualism, from those most affected by it.

From the transsexuals' standpoint, they are stories of survival and as such, should provide encouragement and hope for present and future generations of transsexuals. Perhaps, as the knowledge on transsexualism grows, more understanding and acceptance will also come about, so that more transsexuals will have the love and support that they deserve, from family, friends and lovers. Never before has such a thrilling collection of personal journeys been gathered together in one book.

We present people from all walks of life with diverse histories whose only common factor is that they are all transsexuals. Some are lawyers, accountants, politicians, doctors, writers and members of the church. Coming out is impossible for many, because they would automatically, in some societies, lose their status, income and legal rights, even though to you and me, they look no different from the folks next door.

The majority of transsexuals believe themselves to be normal minded people who, due to the chaos of nature, have found their bodies failing to correspond with their libidos, sexuality and sense of personal identity. This group of naturally occurring people do not concede to being inferior humans or dysfunctioning heterosexuals. In their fight for recognition, transsexuals all over the world are now trying to pressure governments, religion and the medical profession to afford them the status given unquestioningly to others.

We all thought we had learned about the sexes at school, but now here is a compelling and fresh look at the way we classify male, female and all the sexes in between, that have, in the past, rarely come to light. It has been hard to come to terms with this phenomenon, because no-one knew how to refer to transsexuals. A whole new vocabulary of terms is offered to help you, the reader deal with those who can never be classified by the old sex/gender roles.

Never before has a work on transsexualism so closely considered all the relative elements. Anyone who has ever had even the slightest interest or curiosity about this phenomenon will find this book educational, informative and highly compelling reading.

DEFINITIONS AND REDEFINITIONS OF GENDER, SEX AND SEXUALITY

If you look in an English dictionary, you will see that the descriptions of words pertaining to sex are exceptionally sparse. This surely is a reflection of our culture's admission of embarrassment when dealing with matters of the nether regions. It is very important both medically and politically, to be precise in one's phraseology when considering the human condition of transsexualism. Many writers misuse terminology, whether through ignorance or bad intentions, falling short of understanding the scientific and social issues.

Sex

The sum of the characteristics that distinguish organisms, on the basis of their reproductive functions. This is the present day dictionary definition.

Sex change

A process by which an organism changes from male to female or female to male, during a natural biological phenomenon, that enables it to reproduce without the interaction of any other of its own species. This process never occurs in human beings and the term should never, ever be used in connection with any human experience.

Transsexual

One who may begin life as one biological sex, then implements a self-motivated, complete transformation to appear, and behave as another sex. They have an absolute conviction that they belong to the opposite reproductive sex and no amount of persuasion can dissuade these beliefs. The transsexual undergoes many medical procedures to bring their body in line with self image, e.g. male-to-female and female-to-male.

Transsexualism

The dictionary quotes this as: "an abnormally strong desire to change sex". From a transsexual's point of view, this is a misunderstanding. They believe they already are their destination sex, and have to change their bodies to bring them in line with their perception of themselves.

Gender Dysphoria
A persistent discomfort with one's sex or gender.
Transvestite
Also known as cross-dressing, the wearing of clothes traditionally considered to be of the opposite sex. Sometimes sexual excitement is gained from this and nowadays the term usually refers to men who dress up in women's clothes and make-up.
Transgenderist
(See Appendix A Trans-diversity for a fuller discussion)

Belonging to one sex and partially physically, through hormones and surgery, taking on the appearance of another sex while retaining their original genitalia. These people have no desire to be their opposite sex.

INTERSEX GROUPS

Pseudo hermaphrodite (male): a male who shows secondary female physical characteristics and sometimes there can be female organs present. They may behave in a female manner, but not necessarily. Surgical and hormonal assistance can be offered to determine sex. Sexual preferences may swing in any direction.

The true hermaphrodite: one who is born with organs attributed to both sexes. Quite often surgery is performed shortly after birth to determine sex, although the decision may be left until the developed person chooses their own sex. They may be able to reproduce with either sex and have both sets of reproductive organs. Sexual preference may swing in any direction.

Pseudo hermaphrodite: (female): a female who shows secondary male characteristics(virilism), possibly mental as well as physical. Surgery and hormone treatment is offered to define a sex. Sexual preference may swing in any direction.

We would like to make it clear that transsexualism, along with all the above definitions is a very separate issue from sexual orientation, for example a male to female transsexual is NOT a gay man who wants to be a woman simply to fulfil his sexual desires, nor is a female to male transsexual a lesbian who wants to be a man simply to fulfil her sexual orientation. These are common misconceptions, however they are completely untrue.

There follows some new words, used by us, to make descriptive studies of the subject easier:

Pansexual
To take into account the whole span across the sexes, genders, and sexualities.

Prefemisexual (transsexual)
A transsexual who is crossing the gender barriers from male to female, but has not yet undergone genital surgery.

Femisexual (transsexual)
A transsexual who crosses the gender barriers from male to female, having completed genital surgery.

Premascusexual (transsexual)
A transsexual who is crossing the gender barriers from female to male, but has not yet undergone genital surgery.

Mascusexual (transsexual)
A transsexual who has crossed the gender barriers from female to male, having had genital surgery.

Complisexual (transsexual) – either mascusexual or femisexual
One who has undergone the transsexual experience, now living in their desired gender role, having had genital surgery.

Transheterosexual (transsexual)
One who has crossed from one biological gender to a re-assigned destination gender, now having sexual orientation for their re-assigned opposite gender sex (a straight trannie – i.e a mascusexual who is attracted to females, a femisexual who is attracted to males).

Transhomosexual (transsexual)
One who has crossed from female to male gender by re-assignment procedures, now having a sexual orientation towards their achieved, cosmetic sex (a homosexual, new man i.e a mascusexual attracted to males, a femisexual attracted to females).

Transbisexual (transsexual)
One who has crossed from one biological sex to a destination cosmetic sex, now showing sexual orientation towards both female and male sexes.

Translesbian (transsexual)
A femisexual, who when arriving at the sexually re-assigned destination, shows sexual orientation towards females.

Primary Mascusexual/femisexual
One who knows from a very early age that they are the opposite gender to the body they have. These individuals find it impossible to live as their biological sex and begin to live as members of their believed gender from their teenage years.

Secondary Mascusexual/femisexual
One who discovers later in life that they are transsexual. These people may have known from an early age that they were not the gender that they outwardly appeared to be, but fought against the issue, often marrying and having children. In other words they manage to live and survive, although not necessarily happily so, as members of their biological sex.

Psychosexual Genetics
The study of genetic formulations that bear upon the psychosexual behaviour patterns, whether they be determined before the person is born, or develop later in life.

Gender
It is evident to anyone who lives in the West, that our culture's growing comfort with diverse sexualities leads it towards a reclassification of a broader spectrum of genders, rather than just male and female. We are concerned here, in this book with those who endeavour to become complisexuals and how their lives are affected. Amongst the transsexual community, there have been, at times, criticisms from within, about the hierarchical elitism amongst those who pass, undetected as their desired gender. We are considering the whole transsexual phenomenon and are in no way being exclusive or elitist.

Tracie O'Keefe's story

At eleven years old I found myself strapped to a hospital trolley, pumped full of mind altering drugs and wheeled in front of a team of six psychiatrists. Their demands were to know the truth and I had about a one in a billion chance of getting the answer right. For a whole month no one had been able to extract a single word out of me. I was, to say the very least, in a state of shock. Puberty had arrived. Well! Someone's puberty, but I was unshakeably certain it was most definitely not mine.

I had expected, at the very least, to be mildly attractive, and the boy's body that seemed to be developing around me was surely a mistake, if not a practical joke. It was not that I was an effeminate boy, because I wasn't. By all accounts I was a little roughneck with the temper of a peppered mule. No! it was quite plain to me that this was nothing to do with me and I was not going to have any part of it. The psychiatrists, on the other hand, were determined to keep me strapped to the trolley until I spilled the beans, and not just any beans, mind you, the ones they wanted to hear.

I knew I was female from the very first moments I can consciously remember. Don't ask me how, because I can only reply instinct. When I was there sat amongst the toy fire engines, machine guns and Mechano, it was like being in a foreign land. I wanted to play with prams and dolls, pretending to be a mum or Cinderella at a ball. As I grew up no one listened to the assumed delusion of the child of a schizophrenic father. The journeys to the shrinks began at four years old and I was labelled disturbed, backward, difficult and out of control.

Mother thought children should be seen and not heard, and took my claims to femininity as a personal slight on her authority. There was little love, understanding, sympathy or help throughout my entire childhood, I was alone all the way. Now, years later I have been fortunate enough to find ways to forgive their ignorance and inabilities. In the fifties and sixties it was unheard of to have a transsexual child, because no one even knew what it meant.

So I told the psychiatrists how daddy was violent, because he claimed mother had lovers and a wild assortment of tales about my brothers and their various brushes with the law. I could tell they, the eminent panel of doctors, liked this as they discerningly consulted with each other, then nodded their heads. They looked authoritative, pleased and self congratulations seemed to be in order all round.

I was sure as hell not going to tell them that I knew I was really a girl. That was the kind of careless talk that had got me locked up in the loony bin in the first place. It became obvious after that little session that I was here to stay until hell froze over, drugged, tied up, friendless and scared shitless!

Three years later, on my fifteenth birthday, after several short-term escapes, they officially let me out to live in the big, wide, beautiful world. If I had not been mad when I went into the mental hospital, it surely was impossible to have emerged from it sane. During my stay, I had had several lovers amongst the staff, a stint of being hired out to a brothel, a dose of gonorrhoea, and an exorcism with a priest who told me I was condemned to eternal damnation. If this was what life was going to be like, I decided to quietly end it all with one, two and then three bottles of aspirins.

To add insult to injury, I woke up in a male adult hospital ward, connected to drips, whilst a social worker screamed in my ears that it was evil to hate my body, and crazy to want to be a girl. The fruit bowl I cracked between her ears laid her out stone cold, and at that split second I decided enough was enough, and anyone who got in my way from now on was going to regret it.

Out of the darkness came a light, a glimmer of hope – a kind nurse with a Sunday scandal sheet that carried the latest headlines about the transsexual April Ashley. They read, "Glamorous model April was a man."

Stunned into silence once again, it was the first time I had realised there just might possibly be life beyond the nightmare of living in someone else's body. Whoever's body I was living in I was grateful for them keeping me alive, but I was a prisoner. I could see out of their eyes, hear out of their ears, but I just could not feel anything, except despair and pain – the pain of being a child in a body of the wrong sex, terrified of growing up to be a man. I knew the only way to survive would be to grow into a woman. By hook or by crook, I saw that I only had one choice of action, and it was to be a difficult and long, arduous journey, but I had no choice if I wanted to live.

Twenty five years later, I have achieved my goal, and more than I had ever dreamed of has happened to me. I found the treatment I sought to change my body to be the woman I am today. By the age of twenty two I had had breast augmentation surgery, gender reassignment and rhinoplasty, completing my cosmetic change. I have been married to two different men, had a plethora of lovers and sex that would melt the pages of the Karma Sutra. There are times when I have been wealthy and times when poverty has knocked resoundingly on my door.

To survive, I begged, borrowed and stole what I needed to pay for the treatment and help, in a society that was, in the main, hostile to my cause. Today, I am a therapist practising in London's Harley Street, treating people who are desperately going somewhere, but have simply lost their way. I hope I am the kind of clinician that I needed all those years ago, a non judgmental psychotherapist who empowers people to reach their dreams, whatever they are.

I did not become the wife and mother that I wanted to be when I was a teenager, that was not for me. Instead I live with my beautiful lesbian lover in our bijou in London's colourful, gay Soho. Men have ceased to be compellingly attractive to me, as at forty I reach for the sapphic lips of feminine pleasure. It is not ironic that I am now in love with a woman, it is a plus to all the wonderful experiences I've had along life's rich and varied journey. I am happy with my lot. I can be content to sleep and wake up knowing I will have breasts, plump thighs and crows feet sat under the eyes of a middle aged woman staring back at me from the mirror.

My lover Katrina and I create a microcosm of a world where we are the main players, who adore each other, excluding a sometimes kind or cruel world. There is no need for secrets, I am the transsexual woman she loves, and for that I get Brownie points for survival, not recrimination. I met her whilst I was still married to my last husband, and I never meant to fall in love with her, but my marriage was over and she was there waiting. Waiting for what I was not sure and neither was she, but it has been wonderful discovering together. In the throws of passion, she is like no one I have ever loved before, kind, compassionate, patient, tempestuous, wild and exotic. If you had told me at fifteen I was going to be a lesbian, I would have laughed in your face. So who's laughing now?

Under the care of a psychiatrist at Charing Cross hospital, London I attempted suicide more than once again before I got the surgery I sought to liberate me from the curse of my partly male body. The operations were easy for me, the waiting was not, and even now I am sometimes sad I missed the first twenty years of my life. For they are disconnected from me, gone, filed away under unfortunate non repeatable experiences, nightmares that are contained, under control and safely kept out of reach.

There is no doubt that it has been my wonderful circle of friends that have given me the strength to survive and become the person I am today. The words of encouragement, love, enthusiasm, consolation and sheer fucking bloody mindedness, just when I was about to give up. They have been there through thick and thin, a dozen or more people close to me, who have given me the chance to laugh at myself and the absurdities of life. Perhaps way back I did not have the knowledge to survive, but now I have a strength and understanding that gives me the courage to face anything.

My childhood gave me no education, qualifications, start in life or anything but a belief that I was inferior. To shake that off, analyse it, dilute it and learn from it has been a personal voyage of a thousand light years of understanding. At fifteen I was on my own, thrust out into a hostile world in a body of the wrong sex. Just imagine waking up one day and you are in someone else's body. Would that be traumatic to you?

I can't pretend it has been a bed of roses. I have been a cleaner, telephonist, hairdresser, dancer and singer, hotelier, and even the victim of a blackmail plot by my own husband. I have been raped and laughed at by the police because raping my vagina is a public joke, not a crime. By virtue of the fact I am a transsexual, many of my civil rights are invalid and I cannot even be buried legally under my own chosen identity. The inhuman treatment I receive from the British law system, if subject to any other sector of society would cause international trade sanctions. BUT STILL I'M HERE!

Things have indeed moved on. Today I get people from all over the world, of all ages, coming into my consulting rooms, seeking to make sense of their confusions. They range from eight to eighty and there are no rules about the transsexual condition, it is as diverse as life itself. We can surgically and chemically alter people to such an incredible extent that their own mothers won't recognise them. For many, this is what they want and need to survive as human beings, but for others it is not the answer.

I have never regretted one second of the course I took all those years ago to change my cosmetic self to match my beliefs and persona. It was the only course open to me and without it I would have died of the mental torture I suffered. Sooner or later, without treatment, I would have succeeded in killing myself. The treatment saved my life and gave me peace of mind, enabling me to love myself and therefore love others too.

Some of the treatment was of the highest standard and some was of the lowest. My psychiatrist was totally incompetent and cruel. If he were alive today I would do my utmost to have him struck off. He had no empathy at all with me, and made me wait for years for the desperate treatment I needed at fifteen. Both at the hands of him and the medical system I suffered many years of life threatening depression that was unnecessary and inhuman. Some of my friends who suffered the same fate have managed to survive and triumph, but some, sadly, along the way, are buried six foot under, for they were not able to suffer any more of the abuse that masqueraded as treatment.

Still today, many transsexuals suffer at the hands of many dictatorial or incompetent professionals, who are badly trained and often disinterested in their patients' plight. Many of the helping clinicians are ruthlessly driven by profit and have an uncompromising investment in their patients staying ill.

There are, of course, many fabulously skilled, empathetic, kind, happy, humanistic psychologists, psychiatrists, therapists, surgeons, social workers and professionals out there helping. I fight along side other transsexuals and their friends and relatives. These people have decided enough is enough and we are not going take the social or legal oppression any more.

I am a transsexual woman, bisexual, a clinician who is interested in helping and empowering people from all walks of life in many different ways. I have suffered the slings and arrows of outrageous fortune and SURVIVED, to become the strong human being I am today. I cannot say I would not have done it a different way if I could have, but I did the best with what I had. I am happy. I am me.

Being female is important to me and I do not seek to disempower any gender, sex or sexuality by claiming mine. I have a right to be the transsexual woman I am.

OFFER OUT YOUR HAND WITH LOVE AND
REMEMBER IT COULD HAVE BEEN YOU!

Chapter One

The Pansexual Theory

Introduction

Throughout the history of any culture, there have always been witch-hunts. Someone, somewhere, somehow profits when the anger of the masses is focused upon an individual or minority who appears to be an outcast. Clumsily written journalism seeking sensationalistic headlines has often misled the general public. The fear of misquotations and untruths have often prevented the media's victims from telling the real versions of their stories.

There are, of course, a profusion of professionals who cash in on a good thing by proffering information correlated from reams of mysterious statistics, gathered by muddy-minded, so-called experts. Unfortunately, guilty amongst others is the medical profession, who have treated transsexuals as heterosexual deviants for many years. Naturally, under such a bombardment of hostile hocus pocus, the average public transsexual has had the good sense to profit financially by writing the most flourishing and entertaining account of their survival as the audiences will swallow. Being thrust into the public eye with one's very existence hung out for all to see must, after all, have some compensations. The publicity associated with such cases truly curtails the future personal choices and possible earning potential of that individual.

Despite psychiatry being a small part of the treatment offered to transsexuals, it assumes too high a profile. Its use as a diagnostic tool can be invaluable, but the overwhelming consumption of transsexuality by psycho-theorists is way out of proportion with its relevancy to the subject. The first substantial work published with any authoritative recognition was "The Transsexual

1

Phenomenon", by the eminent American endocrinologist, Dr. Harry Benjamin, who worked in the field of gender identity. However, due to the over promotion of its own importance, psychiatry has often misdiagnosed patients. There are those who have discovered in later life that they are not transsexual and should never have undergone such irreversible surgery and bodily changing hormonal treatment. On the other hand, there are those patients whose transsexuality has been ignored, causing them to lead a life of complete misery, often leading to suicide.

When some diagnosed transsexuals have undergone gender reassignment, the surgeons have unexpectedly encountered sets of other sex organs, hidden deep within the body. This causes the patient to be re-diagnosed as an hermaphrodite or a pseudo-hermaphrodite. Such discoveries illustrate that, at times, what seems blatantly obvious to the naked eye, or registers under a microscope, may be interpreted differently when diagnostic skills become more refined. The transsexuals insist they are members of their opposite biological sex, and even though evidence to the contrary may not support their claims, perhaps it is a case of science, as yet being still in its genetic infancy.

No sane member of the medical profession has come forward in recent years to label transsexuality as a mental illness. Further to this, the diversity of conditions in which transsexuals spend their childhoods proves conclusively that social influences alone cannot be held to account. Therefore, the logical conclusion must be that the condition is caused by an as yet unknown contributory factor, which causes the physiology of the body to be in contradiction with the chemistry of the mind.

In history, there have been many recorded cases of persons living out their lives in the opposite gender role from their biological sex. These might possibly, if born in modern times, have proved to have been transsexuals, but not necessarily, as they could have chosen to be transvestites. Since surgery and treatments were not

2

available until fifty years ago, many potential transsexuals simply did away with themselves, undiagnosed. Today, the motivation of healthy profits stimulates the market for treatments across the disciplines, much to the relief of many sufferers from this dilemma. Regardless of the money involved, there are many kind-hearted, gifted, sympathetic helpers, who contribute to making transsexuals' lives easier.

The study of sex, psychosexual behaviour, gender and chromosomal differentials must now enter into a new era of reclassification, in the light of the eventual emergence of psychosexual genetics. No longer is homosexuality classified by the West amongst diseases, having been taken out of the medical books as a heterosexual deviation. Attempts are being made, as we write this book, to treat transsexuality in the same way and in the light of the plausible science of psychosexual genetics, the standard chromosome test should also be re-devised.

The amoeba, with its single solitary cell, is self reproducing. By splitting itself into two organisms, it replicates. The majority of the Earth's animals are composed of the two sexes, male and female. What if the reproductive process was infinitely more complicated than this, involving the co-operation of three, or four sexes in order to reproduce? Who is to say that in our travels into outer space, or studies into micro-biology we will not encounter such life? Surely as we realise our insignificance amongst the universes and galaxies, we must acquiesce to the truth that we might be the exception, rather than the rule. How much easier it must be for the amoeba, without the wooing and cooing of courtship. Though imagine how envious we would be if we were able to see the pleasures of a being who had the capabilities of multisexual copulation.

On the surface of the very planet upon which we live, there are creatures to whom our human model of sex and gender cannot be applied. The male seahorse, for example, takes the eggs from the female into his own body, fertilises them and gives birth.

Sex is unquestionably a process of reproduction, but could well be more complicated than the birds and bees would have us believe. History has recorded the intersex, with fascination in art, as the ancient statue of an hermaphrodite stands drawing crowds in the Uffizi museum. Nature entertains herself, or dabbles with the ever creative paintbrushes of life, not in order to humiliate us, but for her own amusement. In our own intoxicating splendour we make up theories of where, how, and when we come from, which is as much a guessing game as where we might end up. In all honesty, at the end of the day, our collective achievements will not really matter a fig, if God ever does actually turn up.

To understand the pansexual theory, we must first acknowledge that the heterosexual ego is the main obstacle in the way of comprehending minorities' sexualities. Society and the medical profession have both been guilty of judging minority sexualities as heterosexual deviances, and not as sexualities in their own rights. In recent times there has been some progress on this front with the advent of homosexuals grouping together to form gay liberation movements. Bill Clinton's efforts, nevertheless, have failed to gain full protection for military gays, whose absence of rights still contravenes the spirit of the first amendment, in the biggest democracy in the world.

To take the widest possible pansexual view, we must re-evaluate gender and sexuality when taking into account a person's chromosomal, biological, and behavioural (psychological) sex. Therefore, we arrive at a concept which gives us a chart, starting at female heterosexual, and going all the way through sex and sexualities, until we arrive at the opposite extreme of the heterosexual male. In order to progress our scientific knowledge, we must dump the old modular sexual scale based upon Adam, Eve and that bloody silly apple. Such new understandings may help us to go forward into a new age of social sexual beliefs, where all minorities may gain their full statuses as individual groups.

4

In America, in recent years, there has been a concerted effort to prove that homosexuals have a different set of genes from heterosexuals, making obsolete the old theory of gayness by social conditioning. Unfortunately, this has upset many gay groups. They felt such means of identifying homosexuals could be used against them, either by aborting gay foetuses, or by medical, unauthorised testing of people's sexuality, which could possibly lead to selective breeding. Inevitably, as genetics progresses, a transsexual pattern of genes may be identified, just as we may tell the colour of a person's hair, eyes or skin from their genetic make-up.

THE PANSEXUAL CHART
This chart represents the diversity of human sexuality under our definitions. It is not exhaustive and there may be many more – like a rainbow which has seven colours that can be broken into hundreds of distinct colours.

heterosexual male
bisexual male
homosexual male
transhomosexual male
transheterosexual male
transbisexual male
prefemisexual
pseudo hermaphrodite(male)
true hermaphrodite
pseudo hermaphrodite(female)
premascusexual
transbisexual female
transheterosexual female
translesbian
lesbian
bisexual female
heterosexual female

We have not explored the possibilities of such a scale, to its "n"th degree and concede that there could be a call for further insertions to be made on behalf of other identifiable groups.

To classify people pansexually may seem to many a harsh way of looking at sex, sexuality and gender, but unless we clearly define the categories, then it is impossible for each group to claim their set of social, legal and political rights. Janice Raymond, in her book "The Transsexual Empire", attempted to annihilate the transsexual's right to exist by viewing femisexuals as intruders upon the feminist cause. Her book is discussed more in detail in chapter six, "Politics and the Law".

Most reluctantly, the medical fraternity has slowly been blackmailed into letting go of the reins of the heterosexual phobia of other sexualities. This opens up the possibilities, based upon sound logical scientific statistics, that sex is inextricably linked with sexuality and defining one's own gender. Therefore, only by our classification of sex widening to a pansexual scope of view, may we follow the logical scientific conclusion that life is not solely based upon the mythological Adam and Eve theory, which is outmoded and inhumanitarian.

Mascusexuals

Mostly clouded in a smoke screen of mystery, due to a general unwillingness to expose themselves to the public gaze, mascusexuals move amongst us in society, quite unnoticed, functioning as men. They stalk the male domain, living as sea captains, generals, doctors, bricklayers and a diversity of other professions, quite undetected, having been physiologically changed beyond any concept of the female form. Many of them go on with their lives, either as bachelors or acting as fathers in a family unit.

A recent study at the Maudsley Hospital, England by Dr James Barrett reveals that they often move up in the income bracket after going through their transformation and having had surgery to create a constructed penis. As far as they are concerned, they are men with all their plus's and faults, not normally proffering information on their pasts. A generation of primary mascusexuals who received hormone treatment from their teenage years on, have created a breed who are so physically convincing as men, only the most experienced of physicians would be able to detect their origins upon examining them. Not all of them have turned out to be heterosexuals, some become gay men.

Throughout this book we may refer to people as mascusexual when they are physiologically premascusexual. This is because it is unfair not to allow a person to define their own identity when surgery cannot be an option. Perhaps this is because surgery is not advanced enough in this area or because ill health prohibits such action. The same thing could even apply to some prefemisexuals. Let's be honest, we don't have a right to define anyone's identity, we're just hoping to give more options to the vast rainbow of human experience.

There is evidence of many potential mascusexuals littered throughout the history of all cultures. The life of Jack Bee Garland has been presented in a book called "Female to Male" by the American author Louis Sullivan. Liz Hodgkinson records the life of Michael Dillon in the book "Michael nèe Laura", who was supposedly the world's first medically assisted female to male gender reassignment. Marjorie Garber, in her book "Vested Interests" barks on about her considerations of transsexuality, saying how no case of a female-male transsexual, who is still alive, can spring to mind: Someone should have told her about Mark Rees, whose story was splashed all over the Sunday newspapers when he stood for and was elected councillor in his local borough.

The death of Billy Tipton, the jazz musician shocked his family and the world when the autopsy revealed that he was really a biological female. He and his spouse had slept in separate bedrooms, never having consummated their relationship, but having brought up an adopted family, without her ever discovering his deepest, darkest secret. Dr. James Barry, Inspector General of the Medical Department of the British Army, was discovered to be a biological female on his death in 1865, after having been undiscovered in the army for forty years.

A feminine boy has never been particularly easy for western society to take, but a tomboy has always had a much more acceptable passage through her childhood, therefore making it easier for the premascusexual to blend into early manhood, strange as the concept may seem to many. Some become the most handsome of men, never having developed into womanhood, but having gone straight on from childhood to be muscular and masculine.

In the world of male fashion, the image of a "pretty" boy has been made popular. One presumes that this would supposedly make it easier for these mascusexuals to pass as their desired sex. Nothing is farther from the truth, as the majority of them eventually look very masculine. We must also consider that the illusion of the media's portrayal of the sexually active male, i.e the stud, is after all, just that - an illusion. It is common knowledge that the diversity of the male genitalia is far more complex than the porn films of Hollywood would have us believe, and for the majority of men, the ability to actively perform sexual acrobatics is limited to only a certain number of years. One mascusexual we spoke to quite categorically declared, "I've lived like this all my life, I'm sure as hell a man and I don't need a penis to prove it."

Mascusexuals, having declared that they are really men, do everything they possibly can to masculinize themselves. They do not identify as or like to be referred to as lesbians. This is not the accommodation of a masculine woman into an easier role, where she will be accredited for her masculine attributes, as opposed to being castigated for her feminine deficits. They are not within the official hermaphroditic range and should be considered as a complete sex of their own. Not all premascusexuals become mascusexuals, because of the lack of satisfaction in the surgical results of phalloplasty (see Chapter Four, "Treatment").

In the mid 1990s there is the emergence of varying

8

groups of gender adventurers and these can be women who have chosen to live the transgender role. They undergo hormone treatment and surgery to be identified as male, but do not consider themselves to be men, rather as masculinised women (F to M identified). Our book mainly considers those mascusexuals who do identify themselves as men. However, since the gender adventurers' mind set can change, they may, at times, come into the mascusexual category.

Femisexuals

The social and economic disadvantages of being female, in today's society, would surely dissuade anyone from making such a decision about their own future. Women, statistically, do two thirds of the world's work and receive less than one third of the world's pay. The femisexual makes no conscious decision about her future, it is, she believes, the only way she can continue to survive in the body which she is inhabiting. Medicine has described them as males who have a compulsion to belong to the female sex. However, femisexuals see the whole concept differently, believing that they are of the female sex, but have somehow ended up possessing the wrong kind of body, which they attempt, to the best of their ability, to customise, according to their needs.

The diversity of the now public transsexual appearing in our culture leads to confusion. The primary prefemisexual that never reaches adulthood in her original biological sex moves silently amongst the mainstream society, not disclosing her condition. After treatment she goes on to lead a life that might be considered reasonably stabilised as her achieved sex. Often, these primary femisexuals have had their physical development arrested before adulthood, therefore allowing them to develop, under treatment, as convincing women and to become functioning female members of society, totally undetected by us all. Some go on to be models, actresses, recording artists, competing alongside the most beautiful of biological women.

One such femisexual is Caroline Cossey, also known as Tula. She became famous in the seventies and eighties, as the Smirnoff Vodka girl. She was a model who then got a small part in the James Bond film, "For Your Eyes Only" until the press got wind of the fact that she was transsexual. The usual sensationalistic headlines followed and her modelling career was dented as well as her planned appearance in the film, which ended up on the cutting room floor.

Understandably, the public are confused when a grandfather of six suddenly begins to call himself "Shirley", and starts claiming he is now going to be a woman. This particular group of prefemisexuals all have a justifiable story to tell which explains why their lives have turned out the way they have. The author and artist Erica Rutherford gives us her own version of a story of a later life gender reassignment. She articulately portrays her life, in her book "Nine Lives", which tells us of the torment she suffered before the world recognised or labelled the transsexual condition.

Life can still be extremely hard for those who appear to have chosen to disassociate themselves from a revered masculinity. Waking up every morning with a body one believes belongs to someone else, is disorientating to say the least. This is not a choice any sane person would make and all transsexuals, before being accepted into gender identity clinics, have to be screened for sanity. Most transsexuals spend their lives looking up into space waiting for Mr. Spock or Scottie to beam them up. They feel they are spending their existence on a foreign planet, where they are completely alien to the majority of the host species.

Being physically suitable to pass as a woman is not, and never should be, the primary stipulation when diagnosing prefemisexuality. If a person is 6'7", large and muscular, they can still be diagnosed as being prefemisexuals. The condition seems to affect all ranges of physical, social and intellectual types throughout all sectors of society and even though they are a small group in numbers, their origins are diverse.

Not considering the intersex groups such as hermaphrodites, it is physiologically more difficult to turn what was once classified as a biological male into an externally cosmetic woman, than it is to execute the equation the other way around. Certain physical disadvantages can be a drawback. However, bone structure, body mass and superfluous hair growth can be dramatically altered by modern techniques, causing the transformation to be quite cosmetically convincing. Changing mannerisms can be helped by schooling the person for their new life.

Some femisexuals may, unfortunately, find it more difficult than others to acclimatise to lower expectancies of womanhood, in comparison with the higher privileges of men, in a patriarchal society. Secondary femisexuals who may have had successful and lucrative careers whilst living in their biological sex, suddenly find their earnings considerably lower in their new gender role. They will also find it that much harder to climb up the corporate ladder, often being patronised as "girls" or "ladies", and no longer "one of the lads".

Chapter Two

The Possible Causes of Transsexualism

In this chapter we explore the many different possibilities as to the causes of transsexualism. Many theories abound and they are just theories. As yet no-one has come up with indisputable evidence that theirs is the correct one. We have listed many different possibilities and analysed them.

Psycho-theorists, in a torrent of self congratulations, have always brandished this theory or that, to explain away every gesture, hope or humiliation of a person's journey from the cradle to the grave. Clinical, scientifically conducted studies on persons of a so called "deviant behaviour" have continually changed the classification of transsexualism. In their own ignorance, the psychiatric inner circle will go on claiming blazing revelations, ad infinitum. The real truth is, they have as much conclusive evidence as the rest of us, who are thrashing around in a sea of undiscovered knowledge, with only the vaguest of ideas.

Stereotypes

To find a bench-mark from where to begin our explorations we must first examine what is, and what causes heterosexuality. At no time, however, should heterosexuality be considered the standard place from which to measure or understand transsexuality. Is sexual behaviour a matter of instinct? If so, then what is the spark that drives this instinct?

Heterosexuals understand little, as yet, of transsexualism and this ignorance quite naturally perpetuates fear. Transsexual survival is a new occurrence that the world has never seen before, assisted by modern surgery and hormone treatment. Before modern times, the majority of transsexuals would probably have been just another suicide statistic. Once the fear dies down, then maybe the masses, who judge transsexuals by their own yardsticks, can begin to understand that transsexuality lies totally outside the confines of a heterosexual deviancy.

A few hundred years of men constructing theories, based upon their over-obsessive concerns with their own penises, has led psychiatry up a blind alley. Heterosexuality has been slow to learn that it is instinct and not deviation that predetermines peoples' minority sexualities. An animal follows the scent of its mate, after which a full set of sexual rituals ensue, culminating in procreation and humans are animals, maybe the most dextrous on the planet, but they are animals just the same. In nature, not everything is heterosexual, indeed horses, birds, goats and many other species throw up homosexuality. So between the self-styled seahorse, the gay horse, and the subdividing one cell amoeba, it seems the diversity of living organisms is more profound than the world of psychiatry would have us believe.

Animals procreate because their genetically encoded instincts tell them to. At the time of mating they may not be considering the semantics of the nuclear family, or calculating that their actions could quite possibly negate non breeders. Some individuals, in any species show no interest whatsoever in the proliferation of their own kind; this leaves us with the factual evidence, that even in the heterosexual world, there are varying degrees of the "normal" behaviour patterns. At the end of all this consideration, we must conclude that the primary concerns of mankind as a species are little different to any other, based purely upon the function of breeding, feeding and keeping warm. However, as the variations within heterosexuality appear quite natural, then any scientist must eventually concede to the hypothesis that transsexuality is a variant within humanity, and not a heterosexual dysfunction.

In preparing this book we read countless accounts of young prefemisexuals who liked to play with dolls, were too delicate to play football or who hated war games. On the other side of the fence, many mascusexuals told us how they grew up rough and tough, tumbling with the boys. This classical role reversal of heterosexual models is not necessarily as simple as it seems. Perhaps, instead of being a sign of heterosexual deviancy, it could be a sign of a child positively displaying their transsexuality.

Environmental influences
Everything on the planet is affected by its surroundings, influencing both its present and future states of being. Since humans are the most dynamic life form, for good or bad, then justly so, they too are becoming artificially altered by any devastating, supposedly unstoppable momentum of change. Environmental damage through toxic pollution, over-cultivation and chemical misdispersement is not only changing the geography and animal life, but also humanity itself. Our food chain now contains an incalculable amount of detected and undetected mutation factors that are influencing disease and human malformations (physiologically and genetically).

Scientists have reported that the male sperm count has plummeted dramatically, whilst at the same time, the almost indestructible artificial hormones from the female birth control pill are constantly being recycled through all our systems via the water supply. In London Dr. Ginsberge of the Royal Free Hospital, published a paper in the Lancet, January 1994, confirming her findings that a drop in male sperm count in the city was definitely linked to the presence of oestrogen-like chemicals in the water supply, called PCB's (poly chlorinated biphenyls). Testicular cancer has doubled within the last thirty years. Malformations in male babies are rising to what doctors call an "alarming rate!". Deformed penises and testicles are some of the ways in which doctors believe environmental damage is showing up in human development.

The possible causes of transsexualism

The age at which females start to menstruate in western society has fallen progressively down from fifteen and sixteen to twelve and thirteen. This may possibly be due to an over-exposure to environmental oestrogen, as well as higher nutritional and health levels. It has recently been confirmed that there are risks of serious repercussions from too much oestrogen, which can lead to cancer of the breasts, reproductive system and endometriosis. Inevitably, when the pill tricks the body into believing it is in a permanent state of pregnancy, long-term complications are bound to occur, but given that we are now *all* passive consumers, through the food chain, incidents of mutation and malformation are rising.

Chemicals are permanently being pumped into the atmosphere, apart from the contamination we encounter at ground level. Offshoot waste such as dioxins and chlor(from chlorine products) permeate our environment through vapours that settle on the fields and in our lakes, causing unnatural contamination.

A few years ago the British government ordered inquiries to be carried out, when anglers found hermaphrodite fish in the River Lea. The young male trout living near sewerage outlets had been artificially feminised by the chemical waste and toxins being dumped into the sewerage. Five further sites were tested and found to be in a similar condition. Mutations of male alligators' sex organs were discovered in Florida in 1980, believed to be caused by ingestion of a DDT- like pesticide.

There is no doubt that genetic irregularities derive, in many cases, from the effects of environmental damage, e.g. the DDT malformations, Hiroshima, occurrence of leukaemia from natural radiation, and other factors. In further cases, the insufficient knowledge of chemicals applied to the human form have resulted in disasters such as the thalidomide incident. Now many women are having their children much later in life, which in itself can increase risks of genetic damage such as the occurrence of Downs Syndrome babies. What is not clear, is whether any of these environmental factors have had an as yet, undiscovered effect upon the genetic composition of the transsexual.

Social effects
Mascusexuals in the old Czechoslovakia

One of England's gay television programmes "Out" ran a feature in August 1994, reporting on the particularly high incidence in pre-liberal Czechoslovakia, of mascusexuals. They claimed that repressive social attitudes towards homosexuality had induced an extraordinarily high incidence of mascusexuals, who were persuaded that they were transsexual because lesbianism was not generally recognised as existing. Before the sexually liberating social attitudes now surfacing in the Eastern Block, sex was very rarely talked about. There was, it seems, an inordinate amount of potential lesbians who had received bad counselling, resulting in surgery. In fact, the figures released were ten mascusexuals to every one femisexual, however no mention was made of any suicide figures.

Two interviews were shown, the first of which was a classic premascusexual who had undergone some surgery and hormonal treatment with happily received results and he was now waiting and considering the possibility of phalloplasty. The second interviewee was an obvious lesbian who, quite mistakenly, had been offered the appropriate treatment for a transsexual and had, much to her relief, refused the procedures.

Let us knock the social conditioning theory on the head, as it was a popular misconception, quite convenient to explain away many a person's embarrassing homosexual relatives. Puritanism, with its feet based firmly in patriarchal oppression, clambered to throw a pitchfork from hell at anyone whose behaviour threatened to undermine the all controlling father figure. The blame for boys fornicating together behind the backs of society was squarely laid at mothers' over protective apron strings. It was a nice try, but recent child psychological research dispels any notion that learned social behaviour is the sole basis for all sexualities. Educational psychologists studied single and group behaviour of infants to see how their play patterns developed both under peer pressure, and in isolation.

Little girls, regardless of role models, or no matter how many guns and hammers they were given, tended to drift towards nursing and playing house. The boy children developed more boisterous natures, gravitating towards games of battling competitiveness. This was found also to be the case when children grew up playing in isolation, away from their peer groups or heavy parental influences.

The Third Sex

The theory of the third sex was a stab in the dark at explaining away the behaviour of transsexuals. It was considered not to be a reproductive sex, but a sex of the mind. By the invention of this strange, illusive, unquantifiable sex, the establishment was attempting to be free of all responsibility for what it conceived as the deviant behaviour of transsexuals. However, this invention was based on the assumption that there are more than two sexes, ignoring any scientific facts or acknowledging that there may be many, many more sexes.

Schizophrenia

Quite understandably, the onset of transsexualism does immediately make you think about the possible splitting of the mind into more than one entity. For a person with one identity, to declare another believed inner self, can temporarily unhinge the judgement of those closely associated with the person. People do not normally claim to be other than they actually are and any suggestions of such claims can give rise to suspicions of delusionary or hallucinatory states of mind. Whilst there are transsexual people who suffer from this personality splitting disorder, there is no evidence that this is anything other than, *pro rata* per normal population. Unfortunately, the public has been exposed to horror movies like "Psycho", "Dressed to Kill" and "Silence of the lambs" where the central character has been portrayed in a suggestive manner as a transsexual, when in actual fact, none of these characters conformed to anything like the classical criteria required for such a diagnosis.

At the Harry Benjamin International Conference on Gender Dysphoria, the Swedes proffered the analytical viewpoint that personality traits and disorders were more prevalent in the transsexual community than in the heterosexual sector of society. Fortunately for the transsexuals, the Swedes found transvestites to have an even markedly higher rate of psycho-pathology, a fact which will be welcomed, no doubt, by the Norman Bates Fan Club. No analysis was offered of the pathological behaviour patterns often exhibited by the heterosexual majority in some societies towards transsexuals by denying them their civil and legal rights.

It is all in the mind

Such a simplistic diagnosis of this condition which consists of so many multi-complex dynamics, has continually fallen into a very sad and unsubstantiated thesis. Figuratively speaking, all intelligent life can be said to be in the mind. Involuntary bodily functions come from the core of every living organisms' central nervous system. These are activated by the interaction of chemical "messengers", as well as external influences. Experiences stored in the memory banks will, predictably at times, cause repetitious behaviour, sometimes atypical of that particular life form. However, it is safe to presume that we will have great difficulty in storing square eggs in a box designed for the fruits of the standard chicken and the comparative analogy of storing transsexual behaviour patterns in the mind of a heterosexual is equally as unergonomic.

Who's world is it anyway?

Each and every one of us sees the world in our own individual way. In order for us to cope with our

18

interactions with the environment, we formulate our own strategies of information generalisation, deletions and distortions. This is blatantly obvious in our use of linguistics. Perhaps transsexuals see, hear or sense the world differently to the remainder of humanity? If so, what can humanity learn from this?

NLP

We all receive information through our five senses: visual, auditory, kinaesthetic (feelings, emotions, sensation, touch), taste and smell. When you listen to people's use of words, it is easy to hear them speaking in a single system e.g.

V. "It's so good to see you. You are looking so well".

A. "I heard you were coming and it's nice to hear your voice".

K. "I feel OK now you are here so we can just relax".

How we process that information may depend upon our natural abilities and early childhood conditioning. Some people store and process the incoming data through a strategically logical system, others via emotional channels. With the three primary senses, visual, auditory and kinaesthetic; each of us has a preference to receive information predominantly through one channel, to the deficit of the others. Each of us develops our own communication strategies in accordance with how we function. Further to that, we develop a secondary system, in which we prefer to access our own information. Some people store their memories in the visual part of the brain, others in the auditory and still others in the kinaesthetic (touch-feelings) part of the brain.

The way in which we experience and interact with the world can be altered by retraining us to change the combination of our modality sensing and reacting. Whilst this is pure Neuro-Linguistic-Programming (a new and dynamic psycho-theology) and very controversial within the corridors of the old psychologies, it is possible to change a person's sensory experiences.

The co-originators of Neuro Linguistic Programming, John Grinder and Richard Bandler have published many books on this new science, which is built upon observation and modification of human behaviour. People who seem to get into trouble emotionally, often store their self images in the kinaesthetic memory bank in the brain. By moving their patterns to the visual or auditory memory banks, it can help the individual have a clearer picture and sound of their own self concept. This is a procedure that needs to be carried out only by a hypnotherapist or NLP practitioner.

If we clinically examine the transsexual experience from such a perspective, perhaps it might be suggested that a person's transsexualism is a behavioural pattern derived from a strategy to cope and survive. Early childhood experiences may have been contributory in developing transsexual Meta-programmes (behavioural programmes).

Body concepts

Add to this the transsexual's own body-concept and we might be able to perceive how they believe they are truly of another sex. Indeed, the very self body concept may have been arrived at as part and parcel of the coping strategy. There is even the possibility that early childhood traumas may have caused an extreme disassociation, leading the transsexual to reject their own apparent body concept.

Logically then, the clinician should be able to reason away or behaviourally modify the transsexual frame of mind. This, however, is not the case. When behavioural modification techniques are applied to the preoperative transsexuals they fail dramatically to alter the person's beliefs about their own body concepts. All that seems to happen is that the individual becomes intensely emotionally depressed or represses their transsexualism until it reappears later in life.

Although this falls heavily into the behaviourist model of the human self, it still does not explain the often blatant androgyny of many primary transsexuals. Should these transsexuals then test chromosomally of the opposite biological sex, it further still makes a nonsense of the whole present sex test.

This failure to boost the egos of the cross-discipline psycho-clinicians is what leads some scientists to now believe that a behaviour encodation on the DNA structure must inevitably be responsible. Those who have had the misfortune to glance upon the grimacing faces of the crestfallen psycho-theologists will readily admit, they are never quite developed enough to admit their own failure. For such godheads to explain the meaning of life and not have it understood is perfectly acceptable, but to be caught out being unsure of the subject matter is tantamount to treachery. If all else fails and they are unable to claim transsexuality as their disciplinary triumph, they can always revert to the words of the revolutionary humanistic psychiatrist, Laing – "FUCK YOU!".

A mad compulsion?

Probably the most stupid classification ever devised by mankind is the declaration of a person's sanity. The brain, encased in bone and consisting of three and a half pounds of gristle with a little added fat is profoundly, individualistically different in every one of us. Professor Pyotr Anokhin estimates that you would have to add ten million kilometres of noughts onto a one to represent the number of connections within the brain. Such information serves to inform us that the incalculable configuration of synaptic arrangements would be unthinkable, even to Einstein himself.

Each and every transsexual, at some stage of their lives, wonders if they have gone completely off their rockers as they try to work out the logic of having their involuntary differential between mind and body. It is all too easy for the clinician, faced with an Arthur calling himself Martha, to arrive at the same conclusion too. Psychologically there is no definitive cause to this condition, no matter how many angles from which it is looked at. From every logical level of human consideration, no one has so far been able to categorically define a pattern of psychological transsexual development. The symptomology is easy enough to spot, whether in primary or secondary cases, but the positive intention behind the behaviour is never consistent in two or more people. Indeed if transsexualism were a viral infection its changing identity would be as chameleon-like as the common cold.

Could this condition be considered a compulsion? Perhaps that might be true if it was a treatable psychological state, but so far there has never been any success with this approach. In fact, the transsexuals themselves have no desire whatsoever, to alter their behaviour in any way, shape or form. Their only concern is with adjusting their bodily form to what they believe is consistent with their real identity. No amount of de-mythology about their beliefs seems to have any effect, either in the short or long term.

Mothers to blame
Many mothers, upon learning that their children have been diagnosed as transsexuals, immediately begin to be consumed by feelings of guilt, considering the possibilities that they may be to blame. This is a quite unrealistic equation when we explore the diverse circumstances in which transsexuals grow up. Certainly, many of the behaviour patterns of children are transferent from parental influences, but taking into account the way offspring display their own sexual preferences after leaving the nest, the transference theory has no validity for standing as a solitary cause.

As the foetus develops physically, mentally and emotionally, the mother's relationship with the child, at each stage, heavily influences its outcome. These factors do not necessarily have to be conscious either, but may be relevant, even if they are incidental. Many transsexuals reports how their parents may have wanted a child of another sex. However, a parallel may be drawn with a proportionate amount of heterosexuals whose parents may also have wanted a child of another sex, needless to say this did not make them transsexual.

There are cases where a child has been brought up as the opposite sex, when the parent had wanted a child of a different sex. Usually the real sex exerts itself in adolescence, although we did hear of a couple who tried to have their fourteen year old son operated on against his wishes. The child was distraught and unable to comprehend what was happening to him.

During the writing of the book Tracie came across a stage hypnotist who, as part of his distasteful act, suggested to a subject that he had lost his penis. The subject, deep in trance, was in full belief of the suggestion and became exceptionally distraught and upset. After the show the stage hypnotist said that he had removed the suggestion, but we think that he was not as skilled as he thought he was.

When the mind gets altered, it is altered forever and can never resume its previous form. So are there elements within transsexualism of the body and mind altering each other in a continual flux of inappropriateness?

Physical effects

The biological difference between the male and the female leads us to believe that much of each sex's behaviour is dependent upon natural composition. No matter how much social conditioning may be present, if a person's biological and chemical composition predetermines a tendency towards certain behavioural characteristics, then no amount of "guns" are going to change a delicate boy into Rambo, or a tomboy into a ballerina. Being Black, Chinese, Scandinavian, tall, short or having a potential aptitude towards languages is all encoded on a person's genetic memory at the point of conception, so why not transsexualism? A fuller discussion of genetics is made towards the end of this chapter and the beginning of chapter three, "Diagnosis".

Brain waves

As physiological specimens, each and every one of us is a fascinating piece of biochemical engineering, whether designed by a higher life force or having occurred incidentally. The brain, the core of our central nervous system, controls our whole existence by interacting with incoming stimuli and initiating outward responses. Such a complex organ differs considerably from person to person, dependent upon a combination of millions of different aspects. It formulates by juggling many billions of nerve cells into a composition of infinite possibilities and any Darwinian would revel in the potential of its ever changing development.

There are differences between the male and female brain, in accordance with the requisite functions expected from each sex by their natural, biological reproductive systems. Social behaviour can be reflective upon nature's dominant instincts of survival and breeding. However, this is not to say that some of those behaviours must be accepted *per se*, in what is an overpopulated and crowded world. Like any designer, there is a chance that nature may have rearranged a few nuts and bolts when it comes to the transsexual.

Each section of the brain has its own particular function and in the advanced brains of primates, those organised usage's are not only incredibly specialised, but also interdependent. The right and the left hemispheres of the brain are connected by a mass of fibrous nerves known as the corpus callosum, which is, yet again, organised differently in males and females. Scientists all over the world have carried out experiments, trying to determine if the brains of transsexuals are fundamentally different from those of their original biological sex peers. Do the two sides of the brain interact differently from those of the average heterosexual?

Brain composure

At the 1995 Harry Benjamin International Gender Symposium, some very exciting research was put forward from Holland. Professor Louis Gooren and his team

24

showed a small study they had made on the brains of dead femisexuals. It seems from their results that there might be a physiological aspect connected to the emergence of transsexualism.

A question was asked about the possible alteration of the brains through long-term exposure to hormone therapy, but the Dutch had allowed for that by comparing femisexual brains against males treated hormonally for cancer. Professor Gooren did however emphasise that this study was in its infancy, due to lack of dead transsexuals. Fortunately, no volunteers were called for.

Professor Gooren identified a number of nuclei in the hypothalamus, that appeared to differ in size between males and females. The hypothalamus, a part of the limbic (inner) brain, is a control centre for sexual and emotional self images. The nuclei were not regarded as being different in size when comparing homosexual and heterosexual men, but in femisexuals, there seemed to be an ambiguously female brain area. Perhaps these differentials could have had an effect upon the cerebral development of transsexual children between the ages of two and four.

We live in an environment flooded with hormonal pollution so is there an element beyond that foetal development which is responsible for such brain composure? Is there an X factor or even a Y factor that makes some individuals more susceptible to developing this condition?

Reincarnation

Our fears of our own mortality lead us inexorably to want to believe in something beyond the grave. By putting aside our own egos, we are able to consider that there are many things we neither know nor understand. Every sector of humanity has its own beliefs of how many times a person's soul is recycled into the world, or what are the possible vehicles it may reappear in.

During our research, we met a femisexual who was convinced that she had lived before as of one of the hand maidens to the Queen Cleopatra. Her convictions were so profound that she spent the majority of her time at home, dressed in the full Egyptian costume, quite to the surprise of the odd travelling salesmen, in whom she seemed to specialise, on a professional basis. During another book we have worked on, we met a stockbroker transvestite who believed he was Queen Victoria and a woman in a bakery who was convinced she was Napoleon. For some of us, it may be hard to take these people seriously but that is their reality and we cannot really see into it, only through their eyes.

After all, we had a friend who met a bizarre little old lady from Grantham who thought she was once the Prime Minister of England and a fellow from Canterbury who said his best friend had risen from the grave after three days.

Hormonal imbalances

With the variations that occur in humans, it is often possible to pick up hormonal imbalances in body functions. The appearance of male characteristics can occur in young girls suffering from anorexia nervosa as the body dysfunctions. Nutritional deprivation naturally upsets the normal hormonal secretions. In males, a lack of physical development may be present when the testes are not correctly producing testosterone, or when the testosterone cannot act on its target tissues, creating a condition called testicular feminisation.

In some biological females, a particularly high level of testosterone can induce the development of male physiological characteristics. There is also evidence that high levels of testosterone in some human beings can be associated with aggression and behavioural characteristics that could be an integral part of their personality.

So far, no endocrinological disorder has been identified as being a contributory factor towards transsexualism. However, there is still much we do not understand about endocrinology and insufficient research has been carried out on transsexuals.

The possible causes of transsexualism

Hormones in the womb
During pregnancy, the environment of the womb and the foetus inter-react hormonally with the chemistry of the mother. To a certain degree, this may alter and affect the development of all foetuses. Until such a time as scientists have perfected a technique of monitoring the effects on the foetuses within the womb, there will be no accurate evaluation to indicate that a possible maternal hormonal imbalance may have affected the development of a transsexual foetus. Certainly the idea is quite plausible, but due to our lack of research knowledge on foetal development and the effects on its glands and brain, it is too soon to speculate on any such causes and effects.

David B. Cheek, MD, who is a fellow of the American College of Surgeons, the American College of Obstetricians and Gynaecologists and the American Society of Clinical Hypnosis of which he was past president has his own ideas. These include communication between mother and child during the gestation period and during the birth. He says that women who are happy and excited about their pregnancy generally give birth without difficulty to healthy children who adapt well to life. However, these children, he believes are outnumbered by those who are the product of a mother who is unhappy with her pregnancy. His perspective on the relationship between the unified mother and child and the human psyche may well have a basis in future research.

Abnormalities in pregnancy
The profound effects of abnormalities that arise during the gestation period of the foetus naturally could be a constituent factor of the causes of transsexualism. Infections in pregnancy such as rubella, toxoplasmosis or cytomegalo-virus can cause the outcome of the foetus to be dramatically changed. Other contributory factors, e.g. alcohol and drug abuse cause prenatal abnormalities, as well as maternal phenylketonuria (PKU), an inherited disorder in which the amino acid, phenylalanine cannot be

converted into another amino acid, tyrosine. Unless phenylalanine is excluded from the mother's diet, it builds up in the body and causes severe mental retardation in the baby.

These and many other influences are cited as altering the physiological or mental abilities of the child in Philip Graham's book "Child Psychiatry: A Developmental Approach". Graham is a consultant at the London Great Ormond Street Children's Hospital.

General Adaptation Theory
Perhaps there is a possibility that the General Adaptation Theory may apply, where the organism has repatterned itself in accordance with its need to survive. In all cases of organism adaptation, the driving force behind such action is protection and continuation of the self. To illogically separate and segregate the interrelated functions of the mind, body and spirit, which make up the whole persona, serves neither the individual nor society.

Chromosomal differentials
In chromosomal identified conditions such as Klinefelter's (XXY), Turner's (XO), Down's Syndrome (trisomy(21) and other autosomal abnormalities, including Cri du Chat Syndrome, individuals show marked behavioural traits considered abnormal or retarded. However, with transsexualism, as with homosexuality, no noted chromosomal deviations have as yet been identified and recorded, enabling a test to be devised. There has been research carried out along these lines, but so far without any conclusive or formulated results.

Any attachment of blame for transsexuality being a congenital chromosomal condition is presently impossible. There is no definitive time as to when it surfaces in a person's personality, as it can be either primary or secondary. The early treatment with hormones and surgery, now available in late adolescence, still bears no relevance to those who suffer from a late onset (secondary transsexualism).

Genetics

All life is based on its molecular biology. The human consciousness is not an entity over which any individual or group, has so far, had a creative patent. "I think therefore I am" is not a conscious thought that has been initiated by one's own desires, it is simply a happening and an awareness. Neither Einstein nor Stephen Hawking could confidently determine the exact moment of the emergence of our known existence. They could make the most brilliant suppositions supported by logic and calculations, but could they truthfully account for the moments that went before?

We are not the Godlike creatures we lead ourselves to believe. All life happens according to the genetic information carried predetermined on its genes; this is not to say that we cannot alter the genetic composition, if we want to. In the USA, the public announcement that geneticists had identified a gene configuration, possibly common to some homosexual males, met with outcries of homophobic persecution.

Recently, due to fears of selective breeding, not only gays but blacks and other minorities also believe that this kind of research may potentially lead to the attempted creation of Hitler's dream of the pure Aryan race.

Behavioural genetics becomes apparent when we consider the cases of some sets of identical twins who were separated at birth, only to be reunited later in life. Possessing replicate sets of genes and not, during the separation, having been subject to each other's influences, it was found that they possessed similar interests, professions, attitudes and social status. This is an obvious example of the probabilities of the mapped out existence of behavioural genetics.

Dr. Herbert Bowler, a psychiatrist from the Melbourne Clinic, having studied hundreds of transsexuals, admits the patients' real aetiology has eluded him. Whilst he reported that no apparent chromosomal differential had shown up so far, he did suspect that ultimately this would, one day, be the revelation of his continuing investigations.

In his book "The Gene Wars" Robert Cook-Deegan MD, who is currently a director of the division of bio-behavioural sciences and mental disorders of the Institute of Medicine in the USA takes us through the proposed "Human Genome Project". This is the most ambitious project of all time in biology that is endeavouring to recognise every constituent of human genetic encodation. There are estimates of how much this will cost and how long it will take: it is likely to cost several billion dollars (but much less than the cost of sending rockets to the moon or Mars) and it will probably take from ten to fifteen years (it is difficult to estimate because the technology is always improving). From the many mapped out biochemical reference points being identified, it is hoped to go on to map out the information that would be needed to theoretically produce a human being.

Although this sounds incredible on first hearing it, the reader must consider, that no one, a hundred years ago, would have believed we would be flying recklessly around the world in big metal birds. Having identified the entities necessarily consistent for human life, then surely amongst that information must be a greater understanding of psycho-sexual behaviour due to predetermined genetic disposition.

Dean Hamer, a geneticist at the U.S. National Cancer Institute in Washington, USA, worked with researchers from the University of Colorado and the Whitehead Institute in Cambridge, Massachusetts to extend his previous study of the DNA linkage among gay men, to include heterosexual men and lesbians. The research published in the science journal, "Nature Genetics" showed genetic markers on some men's X chromosomes that may possibly have led to them being gay, but there was no significant evidence for excess sharing of any of the markers tested in the lesbian sibling pairs. The scientists claim that this suggests that this particular part of the chromosome is involved with predetermining sexual orientation.

Hamer admitted, however, that the study was in no way

conclusive in indicating that men who inherit these markers will automatically be gay. The researchers came to the conclusion that chromosome Xq28 contains genetic information which increases the probability of homosexual orientation. Hamer is reported to have said that he is more than ninety percent sure that his observations were not a fluke, but he admits that, at the moment, they cannot be one hundred percent sure.

At the Harry Benjamin Conference in 1995 a paper was given from the University of Erlangen-Nurnberg, Germany on the analysis of the CYP21B gene in mascusexuals by PCR-SSCP method. A genetic anomaly was identified to be present in many female homosexuals and especially in mascusexuals. Not only did such genetic configuration produce certain behaviours, but also it could produce physiological characteristics.

Isolating the genetic configuration responsible for transsexualism, may prove as precarious as it would enlightening. Will parents wish to abort foetuses who carry the transsexual gene? Might there be a concerted effort to eliminate transsexualism from the human race to supposedly save suffering, and not forgetting cost? The revelation would undoubtedly present the prejudicial, pious moralists with a dilemma, forcing them to choose between the arch evils of abortion, or transsexualism: a debate well worth staying around to hear.

We will explore the possibilities of genetics being responsible for the cause of transsexualism in the next chapter, dealing with diagnosis, as diagnostically, its relevance will one day be of paramount importance.

From Moses, through Mohammed, past Freud and around the rear end of Billy Graham can be constructed just about any derogatory theory, alienating particular sectors of society, as meets a persecutor's needs. What is madness and normality is dependent upon time, place, fashion or the direction of the wind on alternate Thursdays. Surely the pitiful state our planet is in, leaves one with the impressions that putting on a frock or a pair of jack boots in order to express yourself is quite sane. In fact, surely such behaviour is profoundly sane in comparison with nuclear war, infanticide or genocide.

In Dr. Ernest Lawrence Rossi's book "The Psychobiology of Mind-Body Healing." he constantly reminds us that the organism is a whole and the biochemical functions of the brain should never be considered in isolation. He reflects upon Erickson's (Milton) consideration of psychosomatic illnesses, being that the brain resynthesises itself in accordance with the altered dynamics of survival. Therefore even if the transsexualism is a chronic regression and a form of Post Traumatic Stress Syndrome, it is still a consistent part of the whole. In other words, whichever way you look at it, this is still a **medical condition** and not an antisocial act.

So, is there an X factor or even a Y factor that makes some individuals more susceptible to developing the transsexual condition? Again, we reiterate what we said at the beginning of this chapter, that we can all only speculate at the moment as to the causes of transsexualism and though we will all pontificate with our own theories, as yet none of us have any hard-core evidence to substantiate them.

Chapter Three

Diagnosis

A disease is any impairment of normal physiological or psychological function affecting part or the whole of an organism. A specific pathological change is caused by an infection or corruption of normality. The fact is that for many years, transsexualism was considered as a disease of the mind. It is true that the actual gender dysphoria is debilitating, but if we are treating the transsexual with surgery and hormone therapy to minimise the disablement: then surely it is the gender dysphoria that is the ailment and not the transsexuality. The difference is that gender dysphoria is being unhappy with one's gender, transsexuality is simply to be amongst one of the transsexual categories.

Complisexuals claim to have minimised their gender dysphoria through their treatment, therefore eliminating the large part of the problem. The state of transsexuality never disappears but neither does heterosexuality. Attempts are being made to permanently remove the condition of "transsexualism" from the ICD10 (International Classification of Diseases) and it has already been removed from the DSM4 (Diagnostic and Statistical Manual, published 1994). In its place appears the phrase "gender identity discomfort", which is the actual problem that transsexuals suffer from.

In 1954, Roberta Cowell published her autobiography, in which she told how she changed from being a racing driver called Robert to a society debutante called Roberta. The preface to her book was written by the Canon Millbourn who sympathetically supported Roberta's very early gender reassignment, both hormonal treatment and surgery. He tells how he sees it as a new answer to an old problem and refers to her as "This gallant lady".

In those days it was not a problem for her to have her birth certificate changed on the instructions of her doctors. As far back as this, doctors such as the late Dr. Norman Haire have understood the key relevancy of genetics concerning transsexualism, but today, many societies still treat it with the venom it once set upon homosexuality, denying basic human rights.

Who is what, where, how and when are the kinds of classifications that must constantly be reviewed by us all and we should always be looking over the shoulders of the so-called experts. Unfortunately, moralism or religious fervour often cast aspersions on what is logically, scientifically blatant.

Chromosome sexing

The human and mammal species are sexed primarily on appearance of physical reproductive organs. Should there ever be any doubt then the secondary test that is followed is chromosome sexing. In general, the female carries the XX chromosome pattern and the male carries the XY chromosome. This simple test has in the past enabled medics to decide sexing when physical evidence has been inconclusive. There have been court cases when individuals have been declared a particular sex based upon the results of a chromosome test. There are people who are born "sex-reversed", being physically of one sex but chromosomally of the other.

Normal male: physically male-chromosomally male...XY

Normal female: physically female-chromosomally
female...XX

Sex-reversed male: physically male-chromosomally
female...XX

Sex-reversed female: physically female
chromosomally male...XY

In each case of the above, it is presumed that the person will carry out the reproductive function of their biological/physical sex, although in cases of complete sex-reversal, the individuals will invariably be sterile. When the true sex is difficult to determine at birth, because the organs present may be ambiguous, a decision is usually made upon the results of a chromosome test. If this procedure is not followed, a waiting game can often determine the true sex, which usually becomes evident during adolescence. If a mistake has been made about the sex, it is often quite easy, *IN LAW*, for the birth records to be amended.

Transsexuals are of the chromosome group of their original biological sex. Should they be discovered to be completely or partially sex reversed, then they can no longer be considered true transsexuals. When complisexuals cosmetically become members of their achieved sex, still having the chromosomes of their original biological sex, they are still considered legally as members of their original biological sex in many countries, including England. So a mascusexual, who is physically male and living as a male is still considered as legally female, due to having XX chromosomes.

This becomes completely nonsensical when we consider the dynamics of sex reversal. When the law is applied to marginal sexation, it proves to be heterosexually biased, in that it is based only on a two-tier system of male and female. The outdated physical and chromosomal tests now look to be decisively more complicated than scientists would have had us believe.

Many more complicated chromosomal variations occur in mankind, whether due to natural incidence, or genetic damage. Some of the ramifications can result in conditions such as Klinefelter's, Turner's, Down's and Fragile X Syndrome. In these cases, not only can there be physiological sexual ambiguities, but also mental retardation.

Although chromosomal sex is established at fertilisation, with the inheritance of either an X or a Y chromosome from the father, the first signs of male and female sex do not become apparent until six to seven weeks of embryonic development. These differences are first seen in the developing gonads and are dependent on the activity of a gene on the Y chromosome. The search went on for over thirty years, as scientists raced to be the first to define the gene that triggers masculinity. The revelations by British scientists, of their discovery of a tiny fraction of DNA which triggers masculinity, casts new light upon the complicated process of deciphering sex.

The SRY Gene

The proof came in an experiment when female mice embryos carrying the XX chromosomes were injected with a small fragment of the Y chromosome DNA containing the SRY-gene (short for Sex-determining Region Y gene). These mice grew up as male with testes and male behaviour. The experimental work was carried out by a team led jointly by Robin Lovell-Badge of the National Institute for Medical Research and Peter Goodfellow of the Imperial Cancer Research Fund, who published their results in "Nature", early in 1994.

What Lovell-Badge and his colleagues have identified (the SRY gene) is the genetic switch on the Y chromosome that triggers the indifferent gonads (genital ridges) in the embryo to develop into testes rather than ovaries. Once this event has taken place, then male development follows under the influence of the hormones produced from the testes.

In many cases of sex reversal, it has been found that males with XX chromosomes have inherited the tiniest amount of the Y chromosome from their fathers including SRY. Females who are XY on the other hand, have either lost this part of the Y or have mutations that specifically inactivate the SRY gene. While SRY is clearly the normal trigger, the research continues to locate the genes which are controlled by this trigger, which must themselves each be responsible for at least part of the total of masculine or feminine characteristics.

An eventual logical progression should lead us to the conclusion, that some day geneticists will discover the plus and minus factors involved in predetermining transsexuality. Observations of the genetic formations that take place during sex determination, may in future, reveal that transsexuality takes place at this juncture in the life cycle.

The SRY gene is now recognised as the biological switch that changes the female foetus to a male. Considering this factor, we must acquiesce to the possibility that there is a psycho-sexual switch that activates a person's concept of their own sexuality. When these behavioural genetics are discovered, it will disclose the possibility that anyone, for the sake of one tiny little gene, could very well have been or may yet end up a transsexual. In fact you could all have been TRANS-X-U-ALL.

To turn the game of Russian roulette into a logical systematic equation Lovell-Badge and his team are now looking at other genes that could be responsible for preventing female or male development. When we interviewed him, he told us that their discoveries were in their infancy and there are likely to be many more genes involved and the possibility of psychosexual genetics could very well explain so much of what we do not presently understand.

Psychiatry

The patriarchal institution of psychiatry has taken it upon itself to draw up a guideline defining what a transsexual is. Sadly, many psychiatrists are completely ignorant of the subject, whilst others are in the field for the money or the glory. The deceased head of the Charing Cross Gender Identity Clinic in London, Professor John Randell adopted an attitude of absolute authoritarianism, practically accusing his patients of being transsexual, which completely terrified a number of his patients, sometimes driving them to suicide.

This very unsympathetic attitude afforded him a great deal of respect in his field, simply because it was seen as not pandering to the delusions of demented homosexuals. He did, in his own austere Victorian way, hi-jack a pioneering attitude towards the treatment of transsexuals. This however, does not compensate for the abysmal way in which he patronised his often very distressed patients, including Tracie, condemning them to conform to what were his ideas of stereo-typical gender types.

Before any psychiatrist attempts to unravel the confused gender dysphoria of a possible transsexual, a thorough physical examination should first establish that the person is not hermaphroditically intersex. Surprisingly some people are, even without knowing.

In the main, transsexuality is quite evidently self diagnosing. Much of its presence as a condition relies upon the self aware, external behavioural characteristics. The patient, when presenting him/herself for treatment may have been living in their desired gender role full time or part time. Usually they are quite often convinced beyond any shadow of a doubt, that they should have been born a member of their believed sex.

The older transsexual (secondary) may have been living in the role of their original biological sex, trying to conform to what might have been expected of them by society, family or friends. This may even have been to the extent that they married and had children.

The confusing state of affairs that arises, when cross-dressing in any sex occurs, leads to mistaken identities. Those who are considered transvestites may or may not later develop a transsexuality, just the same as any other sector of society. The causes for cross-dressing must be examined very carefully: there is a very big difference between someone who dresses for sexual excitement (transvestism) and a person who, in a state of gender dysphoria (transsexualism), appears to be wearing the clothes culturally associated with the apparent opposite biological sex.

Transsexuals become extremely upset when mistakenly taken for transvestites, since their motivation does not come from any sexual stimulation associated with wearing certain clothes. Femisexuals are more likely to say that the only time they practise transvestism is when they put jeans on to wash the car. On the other hand, mascusexuals would connect transvestism with putting on a dress.

The key to diagnosing transsexuality lies in the observation of the patients' comfortable awareness of themselves when they are living in their believed gender. For this reason, many gender identity clinics require pre-operative transsexuals to live in their believed gender roles for a minimum period of a year prior to surgery.

Misdiagnosis

When this happens, many patients who believed they were transsexual actually come to a realisation that they are not. They find out that they are, in fact, maladjusted transvestites or confused homosexuals. Often, when psychiatrists do not listen closely enough, they completely misdiagnose the patient as being transsexual when they are not. The telltale signs are usually not in the patients' comfortableness with sex, but their awareness of how they believe others see them and their own self image, physical and mental.

A classic case of misdiagnosis was a London teenage prefemisexual who called herself Mary, who was one of the most glamorous people on the social scene. This very convincing individual not only took female hormones, but also lived full time as a woman, quite undetected. Due to the fact that she moved to America, links with her gender identity clinic were severed.

Several years later Martin (Mary) re-emerged in London with two children and a wife, quite happily living as a heterosexual male. Martin had stopped taking female hormones, becoming a body builder on steroids and developed the physique of a would-be Mr. Universe. He was a well adjusted male who had no regrets, was quite comfortable about his past and had no intentions of living differently than he did now. Realising his misdiagnosis, he reverted to his original biological sex, becoming aware that he had gone through a period of transvestism.

Because of lack of funds and insufficient clinic time, many patients are unfortunately not getting the care and the attention they deserve. Dr. Don. Montgomery of the Charing Cross Gender Identity Clinic (National Health hospital) in London says that he had around three hundred referrals to his clinic in 1993 and complains he had not enough time to afford every one the attention they needed. To help get over this problem and to expose the patients themselves to the wider considerations of their condition, he has implemented a system of group therapy sessions.

Time alone is not the only consideration when analysing a patient's condition. Wrong diagnoses can often be motivated by a fat fee. Doctors are not, in general, as ethical as they would have us believe when it comes to big bucks. Many clinicians assess transsexuals by using a purely heterosexual map of the world, analysing the patient's behaviour in terms of what the clinician sees as correct "male" or "female" behaviour.

Expected gender roles
The visual is one of the earliest and most profound experiences that we encounter. What we see, even at a distance, is bound to indirectly influence us more so than any other sensation. The pretty, ugly and in-between are treated respectively, according to their looks. Though it is sad that so many of us are held back because we do not quite have that look of the moment, it is nevertheless true.

One of the criteria that is used to define a transsexual's suitability for treatment is an assessment of whether they will look convincing as their opposite biological sex. Further to this, there are more tests that are applied by clinicians to determine a person's masculinity or femininity on a scale of one to ten. In a case of suspected hermaphroditism this may be of use, but as a tool to diagnosing transsexualism, it is irrelevant.

Suppose for one moment that an individual was a transsexual and indeed they would be most physically unconvincing as their believed sex role. What then? Are they supposed to be "de-transsexualised" so an authoritative clinician can declare they will be much better off as they are? If the rest of us pretend they are mistaken about their own perception of themselves, will they become normal?

It is a cruel and depraved evaluation of a human being to judge them according to looks. If someone wished to apply for a job as a Paris fashion model, then perhaps the reality of their physicality would be relevant to their worth. However, to apply such a concept to basic human rights merely displays the incompetence of the clinician involved and their willingness to sell themselves out to stereotypes. Whores after all, come in all shapes and sizes, including the academic kind.

"Is it or isn't it?" can be applied to all forms of bigotry. The phrase sexism is not exclusively reserved for the discrimination between male and female. Eastern people find Caucasian people smell of dairy products. The West Indians smell sweet to Europeans. Some of us have big noses compared with other races. Every single one of us in the world has something to offer humanity, even if we cannot be very sure what it might be at this moment in time.

The life test
This is a time when the applicant for gender re-affirmation surgery is required to live in their believed gender, full time. The accepted minimum period is usually one year, but some clinics can require as long as three years. It is probably the most difficult time for a transsexual as they may not necessarily have started hormone treatment, leaving them with many physical disadvantages which they have to learn to overcome. This test is considered justified, as after all, this is an intended destination for life, quite irreversible after the event.

More than an estimated eighty percent of people who originally apply for gender reassignment, never complete treatment, obviously having discovered they were not transsexual after all.

For the clinician it can sometimes be a minefield, sorting out the true transsexuals from the rest. Potential pre-operative transsexuals quickly learn what is expected of them in order to gain the golden seal of approval, that will eventually qualify them for surgery. Many psychiatrists are well known to look for a set script from their patients. When they hear the desired configuration, they automatically recommend the patient to a surgeon. Unfortunately, many patients know the script in advance, fitting in accordingly to the psychiatrist's requirements. Some of these patients who have faked the screening process have lived to regret it. They become aware, all too late, that they were not actually transsexual.

The sad consequences of this scenario are not only that the patient has received the wrong treatment, but also that it proves conclusively that there is no way of telling if a person really is transsexual, other than listening intensely to what they have to say. Doctors often do not have sufficient time to afford a patient a correct diagnosis. At the end of the day, one can only recommend that the patient considers very carefully what they are about to do with the rest of their lives. This makes it sound as if the patient has a choice, that is not so. The true transsexual believes their gender re-affirmation treatment is the only way they are able to continue with their lives.

Self diagnosis alone would be an inconclusive, dangerous path to follow for any individual considering surgery of any kind. Regardless of any amount of knowledge one may have acquired on the subject, an objective point of view is always necessary.

The rejection factor
What about the rejection factor? The people who do not want to continue the metamorphosis to its ultimate conclusion take different courses. Some return to their former identities, having rejected the concept of their

transsexual selves. Others may continue in a state of varying gender dysphoria, usually needing intense psychotherapy. Those who may remain in a position of indecision, almost permanently, are either tormented by their lack of decision or indifferent to it.

In Scandinavia, a doctor had a mascusexual patient who, having spent years achieving their believed sex of male, then decided they had made a mistake. After living for five years as a man and having had phalloplasty, the patient then decided they wanted to be a woman. The second gender reassignment procedure was attempted so the person could continue their life as a woman but unfortunately the previous masculinisation meant that they were not terribly convincing as a female on the return journey.

With secondary femisexuals there can be a noted incidence of reversion, where the candidate, having undergone the whole transformation, then decides they are going to go back to living as a man. One of London's seventies' street culture people, the now dead, Pearl, constantly suffered from a changing identity. He believed that sometimes he was homosexual and other times that he was transsexual. He found himself taking hormone therapy and then reverting back to his former homosexual male identity, causing him to be in a permanent state of flux. This confused individual, unfortunately, in the end, drowned his problems in drugs.

One psychiatrist reported that he had a secondary femisexual whose son had applied for gender reaffirment surgery. The son was agonising over his decision, because he was not sure if he had been influenced by the situation of the parent or whether it was a genetic predisposition that led him to believe that he was really a woman.

Finally a word to the wise: despite the disapproval of the medical fraternity, the only real experts in the field are, in actual fact, the transsexuals themselves. Anyone who is considering going along the path of the transsexual experience should meet as many complisexuals as they possibly can, not only across the age spectrum, but also across the social barriers too.

Bad diagnoses by bad clinicians

Unfortunately, those less experienced in treating gender dysphoria may confuse psychopathologies with this condition. All too often, clinicians who are badly trained fail to accept that transsexuality should rightly be incorporated as an intersex. Sadly, some psycho-clinicians are more interested in empowering their own egos, than in truly alleviating the transsexual's gender dysphoria.

In order for many non transsexuals to begin to comprehend the psychodynamics involved in transsexualism, they try to fit the transsexual into a non transsexual diagnosis. It is, no doubt, useful in helping to assess this condition, to be able to have a framework by which to categorise, quantify and diagnose the true transsexual. However, as mentioned earlier, to try and place square eggs in a box made for ordinary eggs can only ever result in a corruption of the truth.

Perhaps there are those transsexuals who suffer from psychological disturbances, but not all must be incorporated into such a minimal group. When looking at it from a subjective point of view, the clinician must intellectually appreciate that the transsexual lives in a hostile world.

Were they black in a white culture, or Martian in a human culture, a similar feasible condition of heightened awareness would be required, to survive. Some blinkered psycho-theorists have centred on the aspect of aggression that can be found in some transsexuals, in certain circumstances, but they fail to take in the whole picture and the individual's need to defend against attack. The treatment of a transsexual by society is more likely to cause psychological problems or so-called abnormal behaviour, than the condition itself.

The Incidence of child abuse in the transsexual population

There is no doubt that many transsexuals were abused as children, numbers however are impossible to ascertain. A vast number of transsexuals do not go through the mainstream clinics, but pay privately for their treatment and do not enter into the clinically analysed statistics. To pursue any line of diagnostic enquiry that attempts to recover repressed memories of early childhood abuse would be futile. Let us remember that ethically, a clinician should be working towards the constructive future of a patient or client and not be embarking upon an experimental hypothesis designed to quantify statistics.

Therefore, random speculation that child abuse is more prevalent in the histories of transsexuals is corrupted by the mere fact that many transsexual clients steer well clear of clinics which attempt to carry out such studies.

The symptoms of childhood abuse can manifest themselves in a variety of psychological and physiological disturbances and it is unlikely that there is a higher incidence of abuse in transsexuals over any other client groups.

Disassociative disorders

A funny thing is, that all the psychiatric theories, psychologies, psycho-philosophies and a ladies' basket weaving evening class from Penge can all verify their own reasons for existence. What is considered the exquisite ability to disassociate in hypnotherapy, may be regarded as a state of traumatic mental disturbance in another discipline.

It has been suggested by those holding clipboards and ticking boxes on printed paper with sharpened pencils that a disassociated state, due to early childhood trauma, may be responsible for transsexualism. Some men and women in white coats have been furiously busy, trying to categorise transsexualism as a disassociated psychopathology. The obsession of these theorists to section off the whole of the human race into different marked and labelled pathologies and sub-neuroses is surely pathological in itself, even by their own standards.

As each generation re-invents its own solutions to the disturbances of its time, the clinicians of yesteryear inevitably end up with egg on their faces. As Freud emerges as a fraud in the light of his unfrocked, imaginatively reported cures of the middle classes, we must concede that our over analytical viewpoints could be the party jokes of tomorrow.

We all, in accordance with our own needs, disassociate to a varying extent continually. It is, after all, a psychophysiological procedure which enables us to survive emotionally.

The narcissistic factor

Gazing into the looking glass, we all see ourselves, along with our aspirations, fantasies and dreams. This is not to say that we are distorting our own realities into an unmanageable route through life. "To sleep, perchance to dream" is the kind of unconscious necessity each of us enjoys, in order to function in a waking state.

It is true, however, that sometimes the uncontrollable hallucinatory delusions of unrealistic expectations lead us all to be extremely disappointed with ourselves and our lives, in comparison with what we dreamed we could have been. The transsexual claims to be attempting a stabilisation of their own reality and not the metamorphic pursuit of an ideal.

If a person applying for gender reassignment treatment is hoping for a miracle which will change them into a Hollywood Goddess or Adonis, this desire has absolutely nothing to do with their transsexualism. Such pursuit of perfection is a separate issue, which should be psychotherapeutically worked through with the individual, in order for them to function more stably in their transsexual lifestyle and accept their limitations like we all do.

Diagnostic criteria

In considering this section, we have been specifically inconclusive, as no magic formula can truly be presented. The first thing we recommend to clients and physicians alike, is that they read every possible piece of information on the subject that they can acquire. All too often, clinicians with insufficient training in this subject are diagnosing the condition.

Simply because a clinician is a qualified psychiatrist, psychologist or psycho-theorist does not mean that they particularly understand the relevant issues of transsexualism. Indeed, many so-called experts are not only frauds, but also dangerous charlatans. Unfortunately, in much of the technical literature on this subject there is very little written about giving the client respectful space to explore their condition.

The common scenario that takes place is that the transsexual obediently performs in accordance with the expectations of the clinician. This does not benefit their long-term prognosis in any way, but, in fear of rejection, they cunningly bypass the clinician's conscious awareness of what is really going on in the transsexual's mind. What may appear to the transsexual to be a short-term gain does not always transpire into a long term benefit and the whole procedure of gender reassignment can go forth, without the clinician really understanding their client's development and readjustment.

Regrets from those post-operatively, who feel they should have taken another course are quite unpredictable. Some who have fulfilled all the necessary clinical and self diagnostic criteria to go forward for gender reassignment have unexpectedly regretted the decision later. As a clinician, one can never be truly certain what the real dynamics are behind the client's own personal circumstances and can only go on the information that is offered.

Chapter Four

Treatment

Hormonal treatment

The beneficial effects of hormone treatment upon the transsexual population has been indisputably phenomenal. It enables patients to function far better in their social environment, work and personal relationships. Previously dysfunctioning gender dysphoric patients become, to a larger degree, physically convincing as a member of their desired sex. They are able to move through the mainstream of life with greater ease, being made more physically acceptable as a member of their believed sex.

Apart from the huge physiological changes that take place with the body, a mental transformation also seems to be evident over a period of time. The reduction of testosterone in prefemisexuals and femisexuals appears to produce a much softer, less aggressive personality. This is not withstanding the anger any woman may feel at finding herself as a second rate member of society, by virtue of her sex. Women have an ability to be more articulate and many feminist complisexuals may be heard shouting about women's rights from the roof tops.

Premascusexuals and mascusexuals become more assertive as hormonally treated males, getting higher paid jobs, quite a social comment in itself. They also develop a better sense of spatial awareness. As with heterosexual males, they become more emotionally introverted, developing personalities more in line with the male persona.

We believe, from talking to the very people themselves, that the introduction of hormone treatment into the transsexual field, has had a comparable effect to the introduction of antibiotics into pathology. The availability of this medication helps reaffirm the patient's believed sex. Of those treated, the majority felt that without treatment they would have taken their lives many years ago, having been unable to live with what they consider is their sexual deformity.

No other medication so far has had such a stabilising effect upon transsexualism. The patient only wishes to confirm their believed sex and does not want to arrive at a compromise with their primary biological sex. Transsexuals who are suffering from other conditions besides their transsexualism must, of course, receive separate treatment for those ailments.

For many years hormonal therapy was denied to the adolescent section of the transsexual community. This action was over cautious on the part of the medical profession and their tendency to play God has cast many suffering transsexuals, unnecessarily, into years of clinical depression. Psychiatry refused to believe a fourteen year old could understand something about themselves that psychiatrists could not.

This attitude was shown very clearly in Oliver Morse's recent documentary on Channel Four Television, "The Decision". This was a story of three mascusexuals and their search for suitable treatment. One of them was a thirteen year old, called Fred who appeared very intelligent and displayed all the classic signs of being transsexual. However, in England, the "experts" were loathe to prescribe any form of hormonal treatment to him, even though the onset of puberty was imminent. This, Fred dreaded and stated that he did not feel he would be able to cope if menstruation started. Fortunately the Dutch are far more advanced in their treatment of transsexuals and he was offered hormones by Professor Louis Gooren and his team at the Free University Hospital in Amsterdam.

Denial of the treatment may cause severe clinical depression in teenage years, which can ruin the prospects for a person's life. However, yet again we urge caution on the side of the diagnostician, pleading with them to listen more closely to their patients.

In our quest to alleviate human suffering, we must overcome the narrow concepts of male and female learnt in childhood. Integration of transsexuals into society, can only be achieved by helping them to function, as near as possible, to their desired identity. This generally comes about with medically assisted treatment designed to help the transsexual's metamorphosis into their believed gender. The pharmacologists' creation of artificial hormones helps a transsexual to contain and stabilise their condition.

Inconclusive, scantily available studies mean that the long-term effects of hormonal treatment on transsexuals have so far remained unpublished at large. This often causes the administration of treatment to be a matter of hit and miss by many physicians, including the most eminent, who are often experimenting in the dark.

A guide to potential hormone treatment by Dr. Sheila Kirk, MD is available from the International Foundation for Gender Education, Massachusetts. It must be emphasised that any patient would be better guided by a physician, although in some countries, self administration may be the only option. Anyone administering treatment should proceed with caution, reading all the available literature. Advice is also often available from many self-help gender associations, whose members will include transsexuals, their families, friends and sometimes professionals.

Unfortunately, the drug market is well known to be as unscrupulous at times as the second-hand car market and patients can often be conned by all too eager peddlers of bogus hormones. Every patient needs to take on the responsibility of identifying which hormone preparation they will be taking and to look up the research on that medication to ensure that it is not just talcum powder in a capsule or coloured water in a vial.

Hormones can be taken orally in pill form, although injections are the fastest way of getting such an elixir of life into the veins. With skin patches, the hormonal dosage can seep evenly through the skin into the body. Implants can act as a slow release mechanism into the body, over a period of months. All of these methods are dependent upon the preparation and its suitability, in accordance with the patient's needs. A wide variety of preparations are used as each individual reacts differently to each medication. Some patients are more suited to certain prescriptions than others.

Femisexuality and hormones

The desired aims are to soften body and facial hair, relax the muscle tone, redistribute fat, soften the voice and achieve a general feminisation. This can either be done with oestrogens, progesterones, anti-androgens or a combination, according to the particular priorities required by the patient.

Some prefemisexuals produce more testosterone than others, therefore needing anti-androgens to block their male hormones, before the female hormones can have a maximising feminising effect. Certain prefemisexuals react more quickly to treatment than others and a patient's ethnic origins may be a contributory factor in the equation. Nature has made the removal of a black beard much harder than a blonde one.

We cannot give recommendations as to which prescriptions may be most effective, that is solely a matter for the medical profession. Contrary to popular belief, not all prescriptions are safe. At least one has been removed from the market in the past, having been discovered to cause cancer. Overdosing of hormones does not necessarily produce the best results. Sometimes the body's defensive mechanisms begin to identify these substances as foreign elements and start to produce a contrary effect.

Many prefemisexuals react strangely to anti-androgens, displaying signs of depression or unpredictable mood swings. Some surgeons recommend an orchidectomy (removal of the testicles) as an alternative to anti-androgens. The orchidectomy course of action must be very carefully considered, because many people over the past thirty years have been misdiagnosed as transsexuals, only to realise when they are half way through their treatment that they are not.

Body and facial hair, although it will soften, can only be completely killed by electrolysis, which must be done with precise expertise to avoid scarring. The proliferation of spider veins that may appear on the surface of the skin may be removed by electrolysis, laser or other beauty techniques.

The ceasing of cranial receding hairlines may stop male balding, but it is unlikely that any areas affected already will begin to grow hair again. Many secondary prefemisexuals are left with the prospect of a life using hairpieces and wigs or having hair transplants.

Strangely enough, finger and toe nails may become brittle and chipped, possibly indicating a lowering of calcium levels, which should be monitored and checked. Further to this, a decalcification of the bones, particularly in long-term femisexuals can lead to often undetected osteoporosis (a condition usually affecting post-menopausal women which causes the bones to become brittle, the woman to lose height and be in great pain). This has happened to many transsexuals who have stopped taking hormones after gender reaffirmation surgery. Endocrinologists are only just beginning to realise that complisexuals actually function as post-menopausal people, who quite naturally may need H.R.T.

Redistribution of body fat takes place with the dissolving of certain muscle tissues. This causes a narrowing of the waist, widening of the buttocks and the occurrence of cellulite and water retention. The muscular structure of the face changes too, giving the patient a much softer, more feminine look.

Long-term concerns from hormonal treatment administered to femisexuals, pertaining to the heart and liver functions, now seem to be allayed. This is due to results not supporting the previously held scepticisms. Research concerning the effects of transsexual hormone replacement therapy have been carried out at the Free University Hospital in Amsterdam. Venous thrombosis and pulmonary embolism are recognised as problems and it is recommended that patients of forty years and over are treated with a transdermal delivery system, which bypasses the liver.

Breast development is naturally one of the biggest concerns to the prefemisexual, which may take place over a total period of up to three years. Using external breast enlarging creams may, to a degree, help the growth. It is however, to be noted, that the development of mammary tissue in post adolescent prefemisexuals will be limited and surgical breast augmentations are usually chosen as a later option. Femisexuals may, unexpectedly, have late breast development after genital surgery. The areola tends to darken and get larger, though this depends very much on the individual.

The occurrence of breast cancer in femisexuality is only on a parallel with the average statistics for ordinary biological females and may even be less and a regular regime of self examination should be followed.

There have been recorded incidents where certain medics have tried the birth pill as a form of hormone treatment on femisexuals, but any results of the effects have never been published, if even concluded.

Before beginning treatment, patients should be made fully aware that hormone treatment will not turn King Kong into Fay Wray. Nevertheless, if some relief from the agony of gender dysphoria is achieved then the treatment may be considered a success.

Mascusexuality and hormones

The frustration of a man without a penis is one thing, but the fact that he might publicly be identified at a glance, is quite an unnecessary state of affairs. The effect of hormone treatment on premascusexuals is usually dramatic and most effective, adding the kind of rough swarthiness one expects of the male persona. With the effect of hormone therapy, the personalities as well as the bodies of primary premascusexuals change beyond all recognition.

There is a myth that the majority of mascusexuals are of small stature, but this is untrue. The more likely explanation is that there are a considerable number of successful mascusexuals out there functioning in society that have never been accounted for. Androgen hormonal treatment is sometimes only as far as some premascusexuals take their transformation, being unenthusiastic about the previously reported results of phalloplasty (the surgical construction of a penis), which is discussed later in this chapter under "Surgery".

One of the first effects noted, after starting treatment, is the rapid growth of hair that appears on the face and the body. This enables the mascusexual to sport the ever popular male display of beards and moustaches. Male cranial balding can take place over a period of time.

Muscular tone alters, becoming denser and more solid with an increase in strength taking place in body and limbs. The fat displacement common in biological women tends to disappear, but naturally no change in the skeleton takes place. The face too changes structure, becoming harder and more masculine. Menstruation stops, but if the medication is withheld, then the cycles may begin again, automatically.

A loss of articulation, coupled with a greater spatial awareness takes place and yet again, if therapy stops, the reversal process takes place. Moodiness and the male tendency not to show one's feelings often becomes present as an automatic part of the personality. Aggression and forthrightness boost what might before have been a timid person, but as well as being a biological male trait, this may also be a case of exploitation of permissible male behaviour.

The sex drive may increase too. One celebrity status mascusexual in America, Les Nichols, one time lover of sex-goddess, Annie Sprinkle, claims to permanently overdose on his hormones, just for this very reason. Not being a shy sort of person, Les once publicly displayed himself in an amusement park peep tent, claiming to be an hermaphrodite. Not only did he have a surgically constructed penis, but also retained a previously naturally occurring vagina. Ms. Sprinkle reported that she had to finish their affair due to fatigue from Les's profound sexual appetite.

Androgen hormonal therapy tends to make the clitoris grow anything from one to three inches. Phalloplasty, nevertheless is the only eventual way of achieving the full penis desired by many premascusexuals.

The risks of heart disorders increase, along with the possibility of higher cholesterol levels, which in turn may be a contributory factor in arteriosclerotic plaques (a blocking of the arteries that prevents good blood flow). Liver dysfunctional effects of androgens are as yet unsubstantiated. Some studies have indicated that high levels of androgens in pre/mascusexuals may be associated with fatty abdominal deposits.

After beginning hormone therapy, the patient shows considerable relief from what they previously described as confused gender dysphoria.

Whilst carrying out our investigations into hormones we became aware of much controversy associated with their creation in a process that may be cruel to animals. There are groups that give information freely to the public concerning alternative medication. Such information may be gained from PETA (People for the Ethical Treatment of Animals), P.O. Box 3169, London NW1 2JF. Any correspondence to this organisation should enclose full return postage.

Surgery

Hollywood has sold the world the idea that Dr. Frankenstein will make you beautiful, and he will also keep you young. This is only partially true, as for many plastic surgeons, the work they do is not only psychologically beneficial to their patients, but sometimes life saving too.

If ever there was a game of Russian roulette, then the process of selecting a good plastic surgeon from amongst the unqualified and mediocre is it. Amazing as it is, in some countries it is still not necessary to have a qualification to be a cosmetic surgeon. In fact, one of the prefemisexuals we interviewed when researching this book, had a breast augmentation by a dentist, who was part-timing to make up his pay. When asked about the incident, she replied "He'd advertised as a plastic surgeon and he offered to do it with a local anaesthetic. I hate anaesthetics, so I accepted. If I'd have known he was a dentist, I would've had my tooth crowned at the same time".

Several reports were made of general surgeons, who had decided to supplement their none too busy practices by taking a fast, dubious qualification from certain universities. We should all bear in mind that a university degree can, in actual fact, be bought.

We have seen work done that, although having cost an awful lot of money, was a complete and utter cosmetic disaster. A plastic surgeon's reputation should only ever be judged by his work and the results should also be seen to be believed. You would not buy a car without any recommendation and so it is up to the individual to view the work the surgeon has done before lying down in front of him.

Any craftsman worth their salt would have no objection to their past clients meeting their present ones, unless s/he has something to hide. Plastic surgery can be equated to the second hand motor trade at times – after purchase, you are ultimately stuck with the results: caveat emptor (buyer beware).

Certain plastic surgeons are apt to become recognised deities amongst the transsexual community. Only clinics of impeccable reputations should be used, as even anaesthetists have been known to fall asleep on the job.

Surgeons should always be researched several times over before anyone considers surgery. If they do not belong to the pedigree, central, medical organisations, then they should be avoided. It is good for business to be well qualified and if they are that good, they will be accredited.

All surgery is bodily invasive and carries with it risks, not always anticipated even by the most professional surgeon who is paying complete attention to his patient. Due to the trauma that anyone suffers post surgically, a certain amount of body shock may be experienced. This is telling the patient to rest and recuperate. From the hundreds of people we have interviewed whilst researching this book, when it comes to plastic surgery, one clear plain message comes across, "Pick the best and forget the rest".

To hate your own biological body sex (gender dysphoria) when you believe it has been wrongly assigned to you might be understandable. However, to hate yourself, *per se* leads directly to the door of the therapist and not to the table of the plastic surgeon. Transsexuals want to wake up in the morning and see the face of their real sexual selves in the mirror. Should they want to see the reflection of someone completely different, then their problem is not transsexuality. Whilst the surgeon can help customise the body in which the transsexual travels through life, his/her mission is not one of teleporting a person's soul into another carcass. Only the foolish or deluded would ask a surgeon to do such a thing. Any person who wants to be someone else completely and is reading this book, stop now and get help!

Transsexuals have been accused of egocentric vanity in their pursuit for surgery. However, if a transsexual needs several operations to become a contented and well-adjusted complisexual, this is in the pursuit of a cure for their gender dysphoria and not merely polysurgery for the sake of vanity.

Rhinoplasty

This is the most common operation carried out in plastic surgery, probably because the nose is the central feature of the face. Each time we gauge our own self-image, there it is, smack bang between our eyes. The straightening or reducing of a crooked nose gives the femisexual patient a softer look. Should a nose be too feminine and small for the face of a mascusexual, then building it up may give them more self confidence, in line with their masculine self-image. It is quite a quick operation and the patient can either be released from hospital the same day or the day afterwards. The plaster comes off after a week, leaving the swelling to go down within a couple of months.

Ears
It is possible to surgically pin back sticking out ears with quite a simple procedure, leaving the patient with a bandage for a short time afterwards. Since transsexuals have enough physical disadvantages, the relief from this predicament for some has helped draw less attention to them.

Facial implants
These are sometimes used to alter the shape and contours of the face, heightening cheekbones or building up chins. Once implanted, they become an integral part of the facial contours and are quite undetectable. This is a much improved contouring method, superior to the disastrous results of free floating silicone.

Jaw lines
The line of the jaw can be altered by breaking and then resetting it. This should only be done by the most experienced of facial reconstruction surgeons.

Chin reduction
It is possible to reduce the size of an over obtrusive chin by surgical means, thereby balancing the contours of the face. Alternatively, it is also possible to build up a recess chin by using facial implants.

Lengthening of lower limbs
This is a procedure used in helping people with growing difficulties such as dwarfism, and it was used to help a

particular premascusexual become taller. The subject was in his early teens and fully convinced of his mascusexuality. He wanted to be a much taller man. The surgeon broke the legs and allowed the new bone to form between a complicated set of pins. It was a procedure that took four years and gained the patient ten inches, at an immense financial cost to his parents, whilst he suffered a long period of pain during the procedure. Brave as he was, he died shortly afterwards in a flying accident and we would like to thank his parents for allowing us to mention him.

Frontal cranial reduction
This is a rare procedure where the surgeon attempts to reduce the forehead by shaving away some of the bone. In our research we could not actually find anyone who had had it done.

Tracheal shave surgery
The Adam's apple can be made smaller by this surgery and some good results have been produced, although short and long-term voice-box disorders have been reported at the hands of some surgeons.

Surgery for raising the vocal pitch
In femisexuals there is a high incidence of dissatisfaction with the eventual pitch of the voice, after the general metamorphosis. Although hormones may raise the pitch somewhat and voice training add to the effect, some patients may still be dissatisfied with the results. Mahieu H.F. and Wong Chung R.P. of the Department of Otorhinolaryngology, Free University Hospital, Amsterdam, have quite confidently reported reasonable success with their patients in this field. They have found it necessary, in certain cases, to go on to a second stage operation, continuing to correct any unsatisfactory results. The operation consists of shortening the vocal chords.

Face lifts and eye jobs

The endless surgeons and methods employed to carry out this kind of work really justifies a book in itself, but we would like to tell you of one bad surgeon. He pulled a client's facelift too far behind her ears, constricting the correct blood flow and she died of a stroke. Another surgeon cut too deep into a client's face when doing an eye job, leaving her with a distorted squint. Temple lifts tend to give a mini face lift, but unfortunately draw the hairline further back: Remember! "Pick the best, forget the rest".

Rib removal

Some femisexuals have been known to have a couple of ribs removed to improve that hourglass shape.

Breast augmentation

With the effects of Premarin and other hormone therapy, the breast area becomes increasingly swollen, particularly when anti-androgens are used alongside the artificial female hormone. For the majority of prefemisexuals, the results are not satisfactory in accordance with the physicality of a biological female. This leads to a desire to seek artificial breast augmentation.

The days of loose floating silicone are long gone thankfully, as the long-term results tended to be disastrous, with the injected substance wandering around the body of its own accord. It was very difficult to remove, causing inflammation, infection and deformities, driving quite a few sufferers to suicide. These days, the accepted method of increasing the size of the breasts is to augment silicone or salt water sacks into the chest behind the breast tissue.

Many law suits concerning the augmentation of silicone breast implants being carried out world-wide at the moment, are probably going to amount to one of the biggest pay-outs in medical history. A large number of women claim to have suffered the most devastating effects from silicone poisoning, with their sacks either bursting or leaking.

At the time of writing this book the use of silicone breast implants was banned in America, only with the exceptions of scientific experimentation. In England, the medical authorities claim there is insufficient evidence to withdraw their use, as the psychological benefits far outweigh any provable disadvantages. There are also many cases in England of the patients suing the manufacturers of these bags.

Auto-immune diseases such as rheumatoid arthritis, scleroderma and systemic lupus eruthematosus have been linked with higher susceptibility levels in women with silicone breast implants. The evidence has not yet been proved conclusively, as the research has never publicly appeared in its totality.

Free floating silicone

Since you have paid to buy our book, we feel it our duty to warn you again: free floating silicone moves around the body causing terrible disfigurement. It should never, ever be injected into the body or face.

Salt water bags are an alternative but many surgeons are reluctant to use them, complaining that they have a tendency to leak and deflate. Some patients tend to change over to salt water sacks, perhaps when they are having their old sacks replaced or maybe if they are having a second enlargement. We are informed that there is yet still a new kind of sack made from a different kind of silicone being used in America on a trial basis, but no results have yet been released.

It is necessary to have spent at least eighteen months on hormone therapy before contemplating an augmentation. The development of mammary tissue is required so the skin may be stretched when they are put in. In prefemisexuals/femisexuals, there is a tendency for the rib cages to be more pronounced than in the biological female. This causes the breasts to point outwards primarily, but after a few years the weight of the sacks pulls everything into a natural line. It is as well to remember anyway, that too large a breast augmentation may look artificial and over conspicuous, rather like having two footballs inside your jumper!

The operation should be carried out in a reputable clinic, taking one to three hours to complete and the patient may be required to stay in overnight. In some countries the patient is allowed to go home the same day; this is usually a move to be more frugal with the costs, after all plastic surgery is an expensive business. The three methods that have been employed in this surgery are through the nipple, under the arm, and under the breast.

Through the nipple

This is an operation that leaves no traces of scars on the breast itself. The nipple is removed, enabling the surgeon to work through the space, finally replacing the nipple after the augmentation. With this method there have been reports of loss of sensation in the nipple area afterwards and should anything go wrong or rejection occur, then the nipple has to be removed again.

Under the arm

By making a tiny incision under the arm, the surgeon is able to slip in the sacks, leaving very little scarring. This method is reported as not giving a particularly natural shape to the breast and there is often rejection, meaning the sacks have to be taken out or replaced.

Under the breast

Without any doubt this is the most popular and successful method of carrying out an augmentation, as a very good shape is achieved. There are also fewer incidences of rejection. Should rejection take place, it is easier for the surgeon to go back through the existing scar and either remove the sack or replace it. A scar is left underneath the breast which, with time, should blend in with the skin reasonably well.

Occasionally, rejections do take place, but if the most

reputable of surgeons has been chosen, then they will be able to cope with the situation accordingly. It must be remembered that all bodily invasive surgery has its risks. Silent ruptures do take place, often unbeknown to the patient. The signs are possible burning, infection, discomfort, breast deformation or deflation. If this occurs, the advice of a surgeon should be sought immediately for replacement or removal.

The examination of breasts with augmentations is often very difficult using normal clinical procedures, as the sacks tend to block out a lot of the views. A detailed examination must be carried out by an expert in ultra-sound, combined with X-rays and regular self examination should supplement regular screening.

Capsular contraction

This is when the scar tissue surrounding the sack becomes hard and causes the breast to become firm. According to the degree of hardening, further surgery may be required to remove the hard scar tissue. This condition may recur.

As we finalise the book for press we believe that there is a new kind of augmentation floating around, excuse the pun. These implants are made from soya bean oil which is less toxic than silicone and more reliable than salt water bags. They are even to have microchips in the back of them so that all the details of their manufacture, content and augmentation are encoded inside the patient. This data is to be registered in Switzerland and a patient can be scanned and then cross-referenced to the data bank. This sounds a wonderful idea, but we should warn possible users to be careful when going through the checkout at supermarkets, lest they should be charged for two extra items.

The shape of things to come

We tracked down a breast prothesis that was called "three dimensional". This is an experimental kind of implant that is shaped with more contour, multi-dimensionally as opposed to just being a tissue raising padding.

Unfortunately, we were not able to contact anyone who had received these implants, but the medical staff we spoke to at St. Thomas's Hospital in London said that they had had very promising results.

Liposuction
This is a process where body and facial fat is removed by sucking it out with a machine. The cost is expensive and only the most experienced of operators should be trusted, as apparently one woman in India had her lips sucked away by a novice! One of the femisexuals we met from California had purposely put on weight and then had herself sculptured, ending up with the most gorgeous shape.

It is also a very useful procedure to reduce excess fatty tissues around the hips, breasts and bottom area in mascusexuals. Again it is better to choose a clinician whose work is well known and respected.

Fat transfer
A method has been devised where the fat from one part of the body can be withdrawn and injected into another part. This procedure has been used for plumping up breasts, firming facial tissue and filling out ageing, sagging areas of skin. There have been derogatory reports of a calcification (building up of calcium) taking place in the recipient area, showing up particularly in breast screening.

Collagen
Though only having short-term effects of six months to a year, the injection of this substance into tissue areas helps reduce the obvious effects of collapsed ageing skin. Popular in facial use.

Dermabrasion
A surgical process where the top layer of the skin is abrasively removed, to reduce pock marks and scars, including electrolysis damage.

Acid skin peel
The top layer of the skin is removed chemically, and the new skin that grows back is less marked and wrinkled. Anyone volunteering to be the first patient of a novice?

Laser treatment
The advances in laser treatment have been phenomenal within the past few years. With a new generation of lasers, pinpoint accuracy can eradicate threadveins, warts and some scarring. Dermatologists are now able to zap away skin disfigurements, which were treated before with the more primitive methods, such as acid skin peel, dermabrasion and sclerotherapy (removal of varicose veins by injecting the vein with a strong irritant, causing inflammation and finally obliteration of the vein).

Dr. Nicholas Lowe, who practises in Harley Street, in the UK and who is professor of clinical dermatology at UCLA says that the advantage of this treatment is that the precise depth of each millimetre can be accurately controlled.

Laser tattoo removal
In recent years the laser method has been able to break down the ink in old tattoos, allowing it to rise to the surface of the skin. This may take several treatments, but we saw some good results.

Mastectomy
This is a very well practised, normal procedure in surgery, due to the commonness of breast cancer in women. Nevertheless, it needs a very skilled hand to minimise scarring and create a well textured, flat skin surface, once the internal breast tissue has been removed. With mascusexuals, due to the growth of hair on the chest from the effects of artificial male hormones, the scars, after healing, can go undetected. There are, however, some surgeons who make too big an incision, causing elongated and raised scarring which later, not only has greater difficulty in healing, but tends to be more exposed beyond the hair that may be growing on the chest.

We have seen some results from a double circle reduction technique, which was aesthetically very pleasing. A circle around the nipple is used as the first incision and then a larger circle is used and the surgeon works around the space in between. After breast reduction, the larger circle is then drawn in and attached to the nipple. This method even allows for a reduction in the nipple size.

After androgen hormonal therapy, there is a possibility that the breast may have diminished somewhat in size but no great reduction is expected. A double mastectomy is in itself, quite a major operation from which the patient can take months to totally recover. However, in the case of mascusexuals, the beneficial psychological effects of not having incumbent breasts encourage recovery beyond what is normally expected.

Phalloplasty

This is the surgical construction of a penis for mascusexuals. Many clinical developments have been made within the last few years, not only in America, but also in Holland, where this operation can be covered by medical insurance or the country's national sickness system. The diversity of available methods of construction must at times seem more than confusing to the candidate who is successfully accepted for such surgery. Many varying results give benefits or the lack of them, according to the surgical procedure employed.

In many patients, initial optimism often gives way to the abandoning of the construction of their cosmetic penis, until a well recognised procedure becomes perfected. The results achieved by experimental surgeons have so far been both cosmetically convincing but sometimes anatomically disappointing. The cosmetic appearance achieved has been psychologically beneficial to the patients and their lives. It allows them to pass undetected in the showers of the sports club, without anyone suspecting that they might once have been anatomically and biologically female.

The very first mention of phalloplasty in medical history

is by Spengler in 1858, however it seemed to be used with reference to the reconstruction of a penis. Throughout time, since then, there have been various surgeons who have attempted to reconstruct and now actually construct, man's holiest of objects. It seems within ten years from now, surgeons may very well have achieved their goal.

In the paper, "From Peniplastica Totalis to Reassignment Surgery of the External Female-to-Male Genitalia in female to maleTranssexuals" (published by vu University Press, Amsterdam), J. Joris Hage from Holland describes some of the operations he and his team have carried out with differing results. Happily, in the paper, there are references to the procedures as sex reaffirment surgery and not as sex change operations.

Many premascusexuals are afraid of having the numerous operations that may be required. The construction of the new penis can often take several surgical procedures, without any guarantees of success. Even a penis that might appear to be cosmetically pleasing to the patient, might not necessarily function satisfactorily. Surgery is naturally looking to perfect, in one operation, a phalloplasty which is both functional and externally convincing, but as yet this is not an ideal reality.

After time, the hormone treatment makes the clitoris grow in size, presenting the surgeon with more material to work with. A hysterectomy and sometimes a vaginalectomy (removal of the vagina) leaves the surgeon with internal vaginal lining that s/he can employ. The labia can be used to form a scrotum, in which prosthetic testicles are placed. The space where the vagina once was is then closed up. The urethra can be lengthened and a large skin flap transplanted from a donor site, for example the arm. Sensitivity is in accordance with the technique and individual results of each case. Scarring from the donor sites is one of the major concerns but choices of various sites give a patient some options and techniques are improving on a continuous sliding scale.

At the Harry Benjamin conference in September, 1995

there was a healthy discussion of several different surgical techniques from different teams from all over the world. Each team honestly reported their success and failures, openly discussing and debating on improvements and advancements in knowledge. Whilst some clients required the insertion of a surgical stiffening rod to assist in sexual intercourse, others were satisfied with more limp, but cosmetically pleasing results. The diversity of the operations presented gave a very wide set of differing results and each team speculated about how they would proceed in years to come.

One team did report that they had reduced their operating procedures to a one stage phalloplasty, using microsurgical techniques. The many operations that they performed altogether in one session could stretch throughout a whole day, with two or three surgeons operating on the patient. In fact, the team leader, in all seriousness was quite candid about the way they broke for lunch, whilst the patient remained unconscious. Due to the extended operating schedule, they commented on how they moved the patient around after lunch, in order to prevent circulatory complications.

Whilst it is generally accepted that the fewer major operating sessions that a patient undergoes, the better for their health, many surgical teams are unsure, possibly through lack of experience, about going for the one-stop mascusexual sex re-affirment surgery.

One delegate at the conference posed with one of the most astoundingly constructed penis ever seen, which he was happy to show to other interested mascusexuals. Apparently the surgery had been performed in Switzerland costing an inestimable fortune, but for him it was money well spent.

Another story that recently hit the news was of a young man from South Africa whose treatment had cost over £20,000 and he had undergone an eleven hour operation. Unfortunately what initially seemed a success turned into a disaster and he had to have the neo-phallus removed. He told of how he was very disappointed, but no blame was attributed as this can often be a precarious surgical procedure.

The prerequisites for the surgery of each individual are founded on what functions the patient requires from his new penis. Certainly, standing to urinate seems to be high on the list of priorities, so that the mascusexual may move amongst biological males, undetected. The aesthetically pleasing appearance of the male genitalia is of paramount importance too. Quite naturally, for some, the participation in sexual intercourse is more important, but patients must always be fully informed, in advance, of any technological limitation of the operations they are to undergo.

A study of the psychological benefits from phalloplasty, assessed by Dr. James Barrett of the Maudsley Hospital in London leads us to the conclusion that the patients are relieved of many of their anxieties about their incomplete selves. A number do go on to form permanent relationships, but others remain aloof and loners. The overall view is that there appears, in general, to be a greater sense of self worth in mascusexuals, post-operatively.

In a humanitarian form of treatment such as this, we must always remember that it is a man without a penis that is being treated and absolutely nothing can compensate for the loss he has already incurred.

Metaidoioplasty
J. Joris Hage, M.D.,Ph.D from Amsterdam, talked about his technique of enlarging the clitoris. This procedure does not use the transplant of skin flaps from other parts of the body, which, as mentioned earlier can leave scars. He maintained that although it produced a smaller penis, it was more functional and he believed that men often overemphasised the importance of size.

Scrotoplasty
A procedure by which a scrotum is constructed in the mascusexual, using reconstructed sections of the labia.

Urethroplasty

This is the surgical lengthening and re-rooting of the urethra in mascusexuals and allows them to urinate whilst in a standing position. Success varies and some mascusexuals end up being permanently catheritised. Results are uneven and the procedure needs to be fully discussed with the proposed surgeon in advance.

Orchidectomy

This is the removal of the testicles in prefemisexuals, often done prior to vaginoplasty, in order to give the patient a less drug dependent feminisation. In some prefemisexuals, the use of anti-androgens causes considerable side effects, such as depression and mood swings. Vaginoplasty (see below) should be carried out no later than three years after an orchidectomy. After this period the scrotal skin may possibly become too reduced to use in the construction of the new vagina.

Vaginoplasty: Labia – and Clitoplasty

This is the surgical construction of a vagina for femisexuals. The surgical procedures involved in vaginoplasty were around long before the treatment of transsexuals. In many children there are often deformities of the genital region, apart from the natural occurrence of the intersex states. Doctors, over the years, when faced with a new born baby with sexually ambiguous organs, have taken it upon themselves to surgically operate on it.

They usually define the subjects as female, as surgically, it is much easier to take away, than it is to add. There was a case of twins in America, where one was a boy and the other ambiguous. The second child was operated on to make it a girl. On reaching puberty the operated child refused to grow up as anything other than a man and sex confirmation had to be applied.

Many cultures actually prefer a masculinisation, due to their own beliefs, but this is a much harder road to follow surgically. The surgical procedures of feminisation have, in many cases, been carried out without the parents' full consent.

The medical profession has kept many common facts and anomalies from the general public, in order to keep the knowledge exclusive to themselves. The majority of physicians who treat these people do not wish to disturb their own calm waters, driving nice cars, sailing private yachts, living in exquisite houses and gaining healthy fortunes. Fortunately, with the media now reporting the technological advancements of plastic surgery, this knowledge is now coming out into the open, instead of being shrouded in mystery.

For prefemisexuals, the possession of their penis seems to be the worst blight upon the face of existence. A mutilating encounter with a combine harvester would be a pleasant experience, in comparison to the curse of remaining for the rest of their lives as they are. Many prefemisexuals, in a fit of depression, with no hope of ever acquiring medical help, have reached for the nearest carving knife, to dismember their perceived, physical threat to their own sanity. Often these poor unfortunates have bled to death or been left horribly disfigured.

A considerable number of biological and genetic females are born with genital deformities that must be corrected by vaginoplasty and the advantage that the prefemisexual has is that the surgeon has many more spare parts to work with. One of the saddest of all conditions is when someone is born with absolutely no genitalia at all, and even the transsexual in their torment must feel profound sympathy for these fellow victims of fate.

Apart from the ability to give birth, it is now possible for a competent, gifted surgeon in the field, to create an amazingly fully functional vagina for the femisexual. New techniques using microsurgery have revolutionised the surgeons' options, enabling them to construct and fashion both a cosmetically convincing and sexually satisfying vagina.

After orchidectomy, the penile, fore and scrotal skin are

utilised to make a tube for the vagina. A space is structured between the rectum and the bladder to accommodate the new vagina. The remainder of the scrotum is used to form the labia majora and minora. An opening is made above the vagina where the shortened urethra is directed to. The rearrangement of the nerves and blood vessels allows the whole area to be sensitive and responsive to stimulation during sexual arousal. Each and every person is an individual, but the majority of patients have reported the sensations associated with a female orgasm, post operatively. The results are appreciably in accordance with the surgeon's skill and his or her operating procedures.

The creation of an artificial vulva and clitoris (clitoplasty) is yet again, entirely dependent upon the particular operating technique of the surgeon. They are like any artist, all subject to their own creativity or lack of it. It is usually a one-stop operation that can take several hours, but there are still those surgeons who prefer to use two operative procedures.

At the end of the operation, a large mould is sewn into the patient to retain the shape of everything until healing occurs, which will be removed some five or six days later. Hospitalisation and restrictions to stay in bed are usually around ten days, but months of recuperation may be needed as a prolapse (caving in of the new vagina) can have catastrophic consequences. Pain can be kept at bay by drugs, but a constant monitoring of the patient is the only way to detect complications.

Many patients who have undergone the creation of a neo-clitoris have been most pleased and report orgasmic sensation both from the clitoris and the vagina. There is still an ongoing debate as to how much tissue should be used for the clitoris to obtain maximum sensation and cosmetic authenticity. Strangely enough, there are a group of people from some cultures, who, due to their beliefs around the sexual act and enjoyment of it, positively do not want at any cost to have a neo-clitoris. There are still many surgeons who do not offer this service and the older operations where the creation of a neo-clitoris did not take place still produce for many people satisfactory cosmetic and sensate effects.

Colonoplasty

The need to use skin grafts to widen or deepen the new vagina has been replaced with colonoplasty. This is a technique where a part of the intestines is used to form the upper part of the vaginal canal. There is a debate going on as to whether this should be used as part of the main vaginoplasty or if it should only be used as a secondary salvage procedure. A surgeon can obviously only work with the material s/he is given but the true size of a surgically constructed vagina cannot be fully estimated pre-operatively.

The transplanted part of the colon does produce a secretion that assists in vaginal lubrication, but there have been a number of reports of fistulas (an abnormal passage between two organs) and infections.

Complications

Even when complications have not occurred it may be necessary in some cases to re-operate in order to make minor alterations to the surgeon's work. In such a lengthy operation, two or more surgeons may be working on the patient at the same time.

Unforeseen factors may enter the equation and surgeons should tell their patients beforehand, that no sure guarantees can be offered with such complicated operations. We did hear of a bad surgeon however, who had to operate on a patient more than eighteen times and he was a professor of surgery at a university teaching hospital.

Fistulas may arise inside the vagina when a break in the lining occurs. They can develop into a hole leading to the rectum and are serious complications that should be operated on immediately. Should a hole be serious, a partial temporary colostomy bag may be needed for up to a year, allowing time for the healing to take place.

Sometimes a prolapse may occur, when the lining of the vagina dies and falls out, possibly accompanied by massive haemorrhaging. It is tragic when this happens, but further surgery with colonoplasty may even still save the day. The all important way to avoid such happenings is to rest and recuperate completely after surgery, but there are times when this sort of thing is the result of bad surgery.

Clitoral inversion is when it has been hard to ascertain how much tissue to use in the creation of the clitoris. One surgeon told us that it is sometimes a very difficult judgement to make, as a different sized genital area can arise when healing happens and the swelling goes away. Through unadvantageous positioning of the clitoris, cancer can also develop but it is rare.

Infection and irritation of nerve endings may, in some cases be a problem, but with constant medical attention, these are problems that can be rectified.

Dilation

After the formulation of the pleasure dome of womanhood, it is time to ensure good maintenance of the vagina in order to retain its condition, enabling the patient to maximise every possible future enjoyment. There can be a tendency towards shrinkage, so a regime of daily dilation with a surgical dilator for the first three months helps elasticise and maximise the capabilities of the new vagina. After this period, it is necessary to dilate once or twice a week, unless regular sexual intercourse is taking place. The lack of natural secretion glands makes it necessary to use more artificial lubrication than the average female, possibly applying a couple of times during sexual intercourse.

The femisexual tends to experience vaginal, more than clitoral orgasms, due to the physical construction of the new vagina. This is dependent upon the attention the surgeon has paid to the assimilation of the clitoris. Some femisexuals are lucky and have both.

Costing

We found that cost for surgery varied enormously, not only in relationship of country to country, but also wildly from surgeon to surgeon. It is true that some surgeons are worth every penny paid and others are not worth bothering with at all. In our opinion it is never worth cutting costs and going for cheaper options when that may compromise the surgical competence, experience and reputation of choice. The patient would be better advised to obtain a surgeon of excellent reputation, even if it means a longer waiting time to accumulate more money.

We are going to give you approximate costing here in British pounds, because we're Brits, after all and if you convert those costs into your own currency, remember they may not necessarily relate to the costs in your country. Much expense can be saved on clinic location, but one should never compromise on professional attendance.

Orchidectomy	– from	£400 - 1500
Vaginoplasty	– from	£2000 - 15,000
Breast augmentation	– from	£600 - 3,500
Mastectomy	– from	£1,000 - 4,000
Hysterectomy	– from	£1,200 - 8,000
Metaidoioplasty	– from	£5,000 - 10,000
Phalloplasty	– from	£30,000 - 100,000
Urethroplasty	– from	£2,000 - 4000

Due to the surgical complications that may arise during any invasive or constructive procedure, either minor or major, the cost to the patient can be dramatically increased. The increases can be not only the financial cost of dealing with complications, but also the emotional cost of undergoing further treatment. The occurrence of fistulas, prolapses, infections, tissue necrosis, permanent catherization, paralysis, or further invasive or reconstructive surgery may change the course of events during treatment. The majority of surgeons throughout the world require the patient to sign a disclaimer form before the surgery so that should complications arise, the surgeon is not responsible. A good surgeon will naturally endeavour to correct an unpredictable outcome to the best of their abilities. Under such circumstances, some surgeons will offer further treatment either free of charge, or at a negotiated rate.

Transsexuality and HIV infection

There is a percentage of the transsexual population that are HIV positive or may even have developed full blown AIDS. One of the controversial questions around this situation has been whether these people can be operated on safely both from the point of view of the patient and the clinical staff involved. Is a patient who is HIV positive more prone to stress and infection through major surgery? Is the clinical team prepared to take the risk of cross infection from patient to staff during surgery? There are no universal guidelines as each country, health authority, surgical team and surgeon has their own risk analysis to consider on an individual basis.

At the 1995 Harry Benjamin Conference, Bill Robertson, Projects Manager of the Gender Centre Inc., New South Wales, Australia showed an HIV prevention health promotion video they had made for local distribution in the transsexual and transgendered community. He realistically and candidly talked about the high number of transsexual and transgendered people who lived in subcultures and were of a high risk group for HIV contraction.

Many had entered the sex industry in order to pay for surgery. We are by no means saying here that all trans-prostitutes practise unsafe sex, but there is a proportion who do. Others who were sexually disorientated were at risk through unsafe brief encounters with strangers in order to supplement their emotional needs. There were also transsexual and transgendered drug abusers who may inadvertently share needles. His film was very humourous and designed in order to get across the maximum health promotion message through a high level of rapport with little pomposity.

Other treatments
Voice training
The voice is more a matter of tone rather than pitch, since in some cases the pitch may not necessarily rise, leaving voice training as the only recourse. A softly elocuted low voice may often sound more womanly than a whining, high pitched hysterical squeal. Female voice patterns and body language are considerably different from men's. Voice training will sometimes help a great deal, particularly when it comes to using the telephone. Fortunately in mascusexuals, hormone treatment very quickly lowers the voice to a reasonably expectable male level.

Behavioural training schools
These exist to provide training for the transsexual to help them integrate into their new gender role. We watched one called "The Feminine Improvement Workshop" run by Stephenie Robinson of La-Zarus Training which was held at the Gendy's Conference in 1996. As the name suggests, this is a course designed particularly for prefemisexuals and femisexuals to provide help with make up skills and general deportment. Herself a femisexual, Stephenie certainly knows her stuff, having trained at Top Teams Model Agency in Brighton and at the Linda Meredith School of Makeup. The workshop includes practical demonstrations, active participation and discussion. Stephenie advocates having a PMA (Positive Mental Attitude) in order to maintain a healthy outlook on life and all those who attended the workshop eagerly participated and appeared to enjoy it immensely and found it very useful. For details of future courses, contact La-zarus Training, Box 4701, London SE1 4XL Tel. 0171 207 8473 E-Mail la-zarus@corporate.nethead.co.uk.

Depilation
The traditional method for hair removal on face and body has been through electrolysis with the needle method. A small electric current is discharged through the tip of the

needle down the hair shaft and electrocutes the bulb of the hair. This makes the hair easy to remove with tweezers and weakens its growth. Each time the hair grows back and is treated with electrolysis again, it becomes weaker and weaker until its strength fades away. Although this method can be painful, it has proved to be the most successful method of long-term depilation. It is essential that a new needle is used with each client to avoid HIV infection.

An advancement of this method was introduced where the client holds a metal bar in their hand in order to complete a circuit enabling the current to be weaker. Although this is a more comfortable method, it is far less effective.

Another method was introduced in the late seventies where tweezers grasped the hair and the current travelled down the moisture to the bulb of the hair as it was plucked out. Again, this method was not very successful.

As we go to print we hold new information in our hands about a research project taking place at the RAFT Institute of Plastic Surgery based at Mount Vernon Hospital in Middlesex where laser treatment for hair removal is being considered. It is very early days for this treatment which is still in clinical trials.

The plastic surgeon, Mr. David Gault said that the trials were proving highly effective for removing excess hair. Against existing depilation methods the laser is speedy, relatively painless, effective and possibly permanent. The research project is in co-ordination with the British laser equipment manufacturers, SLS (Wales) Ltd.

Counselling
Ninety-nine per cent of counsellors have no experience of transsexuality and amongst that number even fewer understand the psychological dynamics involved.

The concept of counselling associated with transsexuality is very new. Pre-operative transsexuals have rarely received anything other than the often brief eye of a psychiatrist, many of whom have no real understanding of the subject either. Complisexuals have been ejected from gender identity clinics almost immediately after gender reassignment surgery, with little after-care. They have almost no guidance to help them fair well in their futures. The mental readjustment that takes place as they become accustomed to their new selves can be traumatic. A large amount may do well, but many have stumbled from an inability to cope with their new lives. Bitter learning experiences can be avoided with more after-care counselling.

As Dr. Montgomery of Charing Cross Hospital rightly says, that after surgery, few patients ever return to his clinic. In all seriousness, what does the present approach have to offer the no longer gender dysphoric transsexual? Their lives continue along the lines they wished, but many unsuspected problems arise connected with their new complisexuality. There is a space needed for the complisexual to consort, from time to time, with their own kind and share experiences.

To review the counselling of complisexuals is very difficult, since most slip into a life of complete secrecy (being silent), for fear of public humiliation and legal discrimination. As yet, the statistical information about their lives is unavailable.

Mind manipulation

The manipulation of the mind has been attempted through various forms of aversion therapy. A stupidly cruel electric shock treatment was applied every time a picture of the same biological sex as the patient was flashed upon a screen in front of them. This was meant to deter so-called misaligned sexual attractions and was also used in a proposed cure of homosexuality. It took no account of the transsexuals' concepts of their own body image, concentrating upon the obsessive connection of all life to heterosexual orientation. This was a theory blown apart with the public emergence of the transhomosexual and translesbian.

Even more dangerous was the egocentric manipulation of the mind by certain psychotheorists, who dabbled like blind technicians with the engineering of other peoples' sexualities. Hopefully, as a race we have progressed a little further towards a more tolerant attitude in recent years.

To tamper with the mind of the transsexual in order to persuade them, against their will, to become another personality should be classified as grievous bodily harm. Ultimately, in a relationship between the clinician and client, the clinician must make a decision on how best to extricate the client from a chronic state of anxiety and dysfunction.

Hypnotherapy is probably one of the most valuable disciplines in helping re-orientate the transsexual. Other peoples' moral baggage really only gets in the way when an individual tries to come to terms with their own identity. In psychotherapy, it should always be remembered that the patients' model of the world is the correct model.

Hypnotherapy
In such a book as this it would be inappropriate for us to hypothesise on the aetiology of transsexualism through the eyes of every known clinical discipline. However, since one of the authors, Tracie, is a clinical hypnotherapist, we have chosen to include this section on what hypnosis can offer the transsexual community.

First of all, hypnotherapy is the utilisation of the trance state by a qualified and experienced professional in hypnosis, to guide an individual along a path of self growth. Trance is an altered state of awareness that can bypass the conscious mind and deal directly with the boss (the unconscious mind). The unconscious mind is in excess of ninety nine percent of a person's brain capacity. It chooses exactly what should be known to the conscious mind, in order to protect the existence and growth of the individual in the present and future.

Apart from all the bodily functions, the unconscious mind also determines the way a person acts and reacts. One of the most famous sayings of Dr. Milton Erickson, the father of modern day hypnosis, is "You know more than you know you know". Transsexuals, by the very nature of the way their personalities are composed, delete a considerable amount of experience from their immediate memories. Some of this deleted experience could be useful in formulating a life management strategy, if it were to be retrieved from the unconscious memory banks.

The late Dr. Wilder Penfield of McGill University produced amazing results from his experiments involving brain surgery. During a surgical procedure, carried out to relieve sufferers of focal epilepsy, he probed different sites in the brain with a galvanic probe, which elicited one forgotten recollection after another. These were specific individual memories experienced fully by the patient, as if the experiences were happening there and then.

He discovered that memories continue intact, even when the person has ceased to be able to recall them. The conclusion of his experiments was that unless our brains are physically damaged, somewhere within the cerebral tissues, we recall all the constituents of everything we have ever experienced.

Psychologists explain that not only do we hold all those memories, but we also recall the exact relationship dynamics that existed at the time of the actual experience. Those relationship dynamics become pre-recorded patterns that we play over and over again, as part of our own personalities. For these very reasons, some psycho-clinicians believe that transsexualism is a learned behaviour and its origins, long forgotten, are buried deep in the unconscious mind. If this were so, then hypnosis would be the only way of retrieving the deep forgotten past.

Unlike the average person, the secondary complisexual has erected a network of psychological filters in the unconscious mind, rather like a brick wall, to deter any invasion from the outside world. When treating depression, anxiety, lack of confidence and chronic behavioural disorders in these patients, it can be invaluable to use **psychotherapeutic hypnosis** to access the unconscious resources.

However, a word of warning, it is imperative that the clinician has a profound understanding of the construction and complexities of the transsexual mind. The auto-destructive repercussions that could arise from procedures utilising age regression might, unless very carefully selected, prove disastrous and destabilising to the patient. All personality supplementation techniques should be based upon generative or modelling formulas, therefore not drawing on past associated, traumatic times. If past resource memories are used then care must be taken not to contaminate those with trauma.

Should memory supplementation be used (as in Erickson's February man), then the clinician must be very careful not to create multiple personalities within the unconscious memory of the patient.

Having given our ominous warning, we must now say that the uses of hypnosis and mind management techniques with transsexuals can be invaluable. Despite their obviously early life physical disabilities, many tend to develop into highly resourceful human beings. Helping them to reconnect to some of their forgotten resources and develop new ones can be an additional treatment offered during psychological counselling. This emphasis to motivate the self towards a greater independence in the environment would help many who have been clinically classified as long-term depressed. Unfortunately, it has become a common practice within the medical circle, to offer antidepressant drugs, where psychotherapy would be more appropriate.

It is mistakenly believed that patients who have suffered from a previously high anxiety level are unable to go into trance. Everyone is able to benefit from trance work, which has a marked calming effect as the brain moves down to Alpha brainwave functions. Even manic and psychotic patients have gained considerable benefits from being taught how to induce alteration in their brain activity.

The effects of self efficacy and mind development techniques can easily be attained by many of the new age transpersonal psychologies, but undoubtedly, hypnosis, coupled with psychotherapy can be transformational. Reality, after all, can be whatever we want it to be.

There have been no published clinical trials of memory retrieval with transsexuals, although during our research, we did hear of unethical experiments that had taken place by clinicians who had insufficient hypnosis training. The danger to the patient of being regressed by unqualified parties cannot be over emphasised. Abreaction work is often viewed controversially within the hypnosis world and should never be attempted by anyone but an experienced hypnotherapist. Great skill is required to help the patient in retrieving the memories that are necessary for treatment and should the wrong memories be allowed to surface, then the patient may be placed in a state of severe psychological imbalance and danger.

There follows a case history of hypnotherapy performed with a complisexual.

Pamela

Pamela, at thirty nine said she was still looking for her ultimate partner. There had been, since her gender reaffirment eighteen years ago, a profusion of live-in lovers and boyfriends. She said she had been happy with some of them and tolerated others, but none of them had offered her what she needed long term. When asked to quantify what she thought she needed long term, she appeared vague and could only illicit the phrase "A real man".

During gender reassignment, at twenty one, her family who were devoutly religious, had rejected her and only a sister remained occasionally in touch. The family in which she was raised was quite unstable with the mother having a religious devotion and the father having disappeared. She had felt, from her earliest recollections, that she was female and rejected out of hand any maleness she had ever known.

She was regarded as classically beautiful in her achieved desired gender role. Due to the instability of her background, she had not gone onto higher education and had spent the majority of her working life in nightclubs as a barmaid. Her present boyfriend was a taxi driver, for whom she did not have a great deal of respect, but when asked why she stayed with him, she replied "Well, what decent man is going to want a girl like me? As soon as they find out what I am, they're off getting some girl pregnant."

Her sisters were close to their mother, all having the common interest of children and grandchildren. Pamela felt quite left out and isolated about her inability to function biologically as a normal female. She seemed to suffer from a core central belief that, due to her transsexualism, she was not good enough to be female.

During bouts of depression, she was subject to heroin addiction, amphetamine and barbiturate abuse. These were common even before she had gender reassignment. She said "It's not that it helps me cope, it's just that it helps block things out for a while." When she was not under the influence of drugs, her social skills and amiability made her very popular, but during drug episodes, she lost all sense of time, self worth and had a total amnesia of her anti-social behaviour after the event.

As an adult, she felt she had coped the best she could with the situation she had, but things had not gone the way she might have liked. The pattern of her life had led to a very transient existence with a need to change her friends every couple of years.

When coming into therapy, she expressed facial contortions and eye fixation on the floor, when trying to talk about her emotions. There were few people to whom she felt she could talk about her innermost needs and aspirations. Indeed, other complisexuals were the very last people she believed wanted to hear about her struggle to survive. She spoke of a bravado amongst them as they sought to display to each other their ability to adjust to their new lives. "It's a tough world", she said, "And you've just got to get on with it, because at the end of the day, you're on your own and nobody truly gives a damn. My mother never forgave me for being who I am and she just feels that I brought shame on her."

After surgery, Pamela had received no psychotherapy, counselling or assistance to readjust to her new life and there had been no family connections where she might seek advice when she needed it. This sense of ostracisation and isolation seemed to be a large contributory factor into her entering into very withdrawn states. She seemed to measure her own success as a person by using the external references of boyfriends and men, in an attempt to validate her own personal worth. She had attempted suicide several times since her treatment and usually whilst in a drug induced state.

When asked what she thought she wanted from therapy, she took a long time to reply and then tentatively and sheepishly asked if more control over her life would be okay. Hypnotherapy was used and it took several sessions to train her to develop a medium hypnotic trance. Her heightened sense of conscious awareness seemed to be a constant vigil that was part of her waking defence mechanism. Only Ericksonian indirect suggestion was used, in order not to encounter any conscious resistance, that might have been perceived as judgmental authoritarianism. On the seventh session, reacting to previously embedded post hypnotic suggestions, she went deeply into a waking somnambulistic trance and I was able to converse with her, on an unconscious level.

It became apparent that she had had no role models in her life, on which to base her own personality and her low self esteem had only allowed her to have a strategy of surviving from disaster to disaster. Due to the repetitive expectations of failure that punctuated her life, the next waiting disaster only seemed to be a simple matter of self efficacy.

I decided to use an interrupter pattern to attempt to break her self fulfilling prophecies. All work was done at a deep unconscious level to avoid any conscious resistance. She was instructed to carry out a daily routine of polishing all the mirrors in her flat, after breakfast, before she utilised a thirty minute trance period. During the trance period, she would listen to a tape, which contained indirect suggestion, concerning the success of her looks and transformation, interspersed with questions about how lucky someone would be to have her as a partner. The trans-derivational questioning was designed for her to synthesise associations about her own self worth.

After a month and several sessions later, her daily tape was changed to one purely based on confidence building and ego strengthening. During the meantime, in therapy, she had learned to look at the earlier periods in her life from an adult perspective and later transmigrated new found abilities into her past memories of herself. (Change personal history – NLP technique, based on the Erickson "February Man" case, where the client is regressed and their memories are supplemented with good, resourceful experiences).

Psycho-imagination techniques were also used to help her synthesise the kind of vision of herself in the future, that she would like. After five weeks, she was going into trance, on a daily basis, happily by herself, without the assistance of any tapes, becoming more autonomous as a personality. Her visits were reduced to once every two weeks for three months, during which, sometimes she went into trance to do more ego strengthening work and sometimes the session was simply counselling while she talked over consciously her life skills. On last hearing of her, she was living alone, quite stable, with a new puppy, occasionally seeing a carpenter she had met, but was not prepared to throw herself into any relationship on the spur of the moment. She continues to use trance each morning after breakfast, which is now the interrupter pattern in itself to her old mode of behaviour.

By exploring and changing her beliefs about her own sense of worth, she was able to change the way she related to herself and the world. This strengthened her ego state, giving her more autonomous self references, as opposed to comparing herself against the functions of biological females.

Complisexual management

When trying to understand and balance the complisexual's long-term survival system, we must first realise that all such people have a late altered development or restructured personality. Transsexuals' mental processes are in a state of prolonged shock, from the time they discover their plight, until some time after their gender realignment.

Whilst the rest of the world may be very supportive and sympathetic, it is impossible for them to truly comprehend the complex altered reality that the transsexual structures, in order to cope with their own integration into the remainder of society. Many are able to acclimatise well into the thrux of mainstream society, often becoming high achievers and happy, contented human beings. Others may find relationships too fractious, preferring to lead a life of isolation.

As primary transsexuals reach their teenage years, beginning to seek help for what they perceive as a routeless path out of their maze, courting, education and personal development suddenly become partly suspended. Their contemporaries are all busy dating, motivated by a newly found sexual libido, from which the transsexual is excluded by the nature of their gender dysphoria.

Feelings of rejection and isolation, coupled with anger, can accompany a sense of guilt that they are somehow responsible for their undesirable state.

Any partner at this stage is likely to be temporary, being under peer pressure themselves to complete some of the generally expected heterosexual adolescent conquests and achievements.

Education is likely to stop. The transsexual may feel extremely uncomfortable around their contemporaries at this stage. They see others accomplishing in so many areas of life, further magnifying the transsexual's perception of their own inadequacies.

Taking into account the effects of the prior two considerations, it is hardly surprising that a mad dash is usually made towards the nearest available sub-culture. Here, the transsexual often finds solace in the company of a number of society's other oddballs.

Primary transsexuals are often unable to assimilate into society until they are able to re-orientate in their desired identity. Only the most understanding and supportive of parents will be able to keep these offspring at home. Any family hostility is interpreted as a cruel stick with which to damage an already suffering and disorientated personality.

Prompt treatment and assistance for the primary transsexual eases the burden of shifting their life's course so dramatically. If a person truly is a transsexual, then there is nothing that any heavy-handed authoritarian can do that will alter that person's mind. All anyone may do is assist the patient to achieve what they need for their continued survival as a human being.

As the metamorphosis takes place, then and only then, will the altered late development of the individual construct a personality that will suffice to help them to travel through life. It will be a very complex personality. Multi-layered subconscious defence mechanisms will operate on an extraordinary high level of awareness. Any attempts to alter or stabilise the transsexual psyche should only be attempted by a clinician who is experienced in working in the field.

The secondary complisexual will arrive at a reconstructed personality after a great deal of torment and self dissemination. As with nervous breakdowns or events of great circumstantial change, e.g. physical, emotional or environmental, the secondary transsexual has to rebuild a life that has already steered a previous course. Their whole prior view of the world is likely to be unrecognisably different.

The changing of an already existing gender naturally re-focuses a person's perceptions. It must be understood that if these patients are correctly diagnosed as true transsexuals, then there is little anyone can do to deter them from their future intended course. Due to the added complicated defence mechanisms that the secondary transsexual constructs subconsciously, the clinician must have a great respect for the psychological dynamics involved.

There are many calls throughout the world from some hierarchies of psychiatry that transsexuals should be excluded as psychological clinicians involved in the transsexual condition. This is quite wrong, as intuitively, professional transsexual clinicians are more likely to understand the transsexual personality. Total control by the mind-manipulating establishment is nothing new from those who base their entire ethos on the social importance of an over-evaluated heterosexuality.

New clinics need to be set up, specifically dealing with the problems of the post operative transsexual. At the moment, only a hotchpotch of non specialist help is available to those who are very desperate or suicidal.

Rebuilding bigger, better trannies

When moving into a new house, it helps to know where the utilities are located, but when moving into a new body, the required necessities are much more complicated. Fortunately, the human brain is one of the most fascinating pieces of engineering on the planet, which appears to be able to inexplicably adapt to almost any situation.

The many therapies that cognitively re-examine thought, in order to make sense of a person's confusion, often lead to unnecessary prolonged distress. If you know you have a broken leg, it is not necessary to keep standing on it to verify the fact. Surely, the better course of action would be to find other options that will eventually lead to well being.

To spend a fortune on altering the transsexual's body, without offering them mental readjustment assistance seems an illogical bias. Many complisexuals, after hormone treatment and a series of operations, still continue to remain dysfunctional human beings within society. Such a statement may sound outrageously judgmental to many, who would be right in opposing any mandatory counselling. However, "the operate and wish for the best" approach has quite plainly, not worked for many patients.

Confidence building through ego strengthening techniques can and does cause dramatic shifts in the depressed personality, leading to a greater sense of holistic well being. There is no doubt that certain sectors of the medical profession view the confident, controlled, complisexual as having an unclassifiable air of psychosis about them. This however, derives from those sectors' insecurities, brought on by their inability to rationalise and understand the complisexuals' reality. After all, let us remember that even the development of cognitive psychology was financed by the CIA, in order to develop human beings as killing machines.

Best utilisation is made of such psychotherapies as Neuro-Linguistic-Programming, where positive mental programming is built on the individual's reality, without interpreting it through an assumed standard model of how it should be. Where the patient does not have the resources, they can model the required abilities from those who are capable of them. "To be or not to be?", should really not be the questions, but how to be and not to be and any other options that you can think of. Every complisexual should be issued with a copy of "Unlimited Power" by Anthony Robbins, a starting gun, and a packet of dextrose glucose sweets as they are wheeled out of the operating theatre. "ON YOUR MARKS-GET SET-GO!"

Chapter Five

Living as a Transsexual

Since humanity got past the eat, drink, fart and sleep stage of social development, transsexuality became part, no matter how small, of the human equation. At the E.N.P.T. Conference (see Appendix C) in Manchester 1994, a clinical psychiatrist from the North of England tried to put forward that perhaps this was a modern day phenomenon. He personally had not come across it in his history books (the English education system is not what it was). If we look very carefully, all the telltale signs are there with the poems of Catullus, the whores of Rome, and the Beaumonts of French society. These references occurred right up until 1945 when the first recorded application was lodged in Switzerland to change a transsexual's identity.

Public transsexuals

Since the Christine Jorgenson case in the fifties (one of the first transsexuals to become public knowledge), many transsexuals have gone to ground. They have seen, all too well, how the attentions of the media were able to turn any hope of a peaceful life into a three-ringed circus. As mentioned earlier in the book, in the eighties, the Smirnoff model, Tula (Caroline Cossey) woke up one morning to find all her private life splashed across the newspapers and her exposure as being a transsexual cost her a modelling career. Overnight, she had changed in the public's eye from being a beautiful supermodel to a freak.

After the trauma of such public humiliation, Tula refused to take it lying down and took her case to the European Court of Rights in Strasbourg to try to get her birth certificate changed so she could legally marry and adopt children in this country. Tragically, they denied her this right and to this day, anyone trying to change their birth certificate is referred to the *Cossey* versus *United Kingdom* case. Devastated at this decision, Tula left England to live in America where she was able to legally change her birth certificate and get married to her present husband. Her sister agreed to carry a baby for her and as far as we know she is living happily as a wife and mother in the USA.

Mark Rees, the mascusexual from the South of England, who evidently could not be treated as a woman by society, was publicly humiliated by the church when they refused to treat him as a man. He was a devout attendee and warder of the church who dedicated much time and effort to the community. However, the general Synod of the Church of England at that time declined entrance to the priesthood to him, because of his original biological sex. Mark is now a local councillor in the government and what seems to be their gain is obviously the church's loss.

In the British gay magazine, "Attitude", November 1995, there was a large article on Europe's queen of disco music, Amanda Lear. It pontificated that the very beautiful, famous, rich recording artist had spent her career eluding the question of whether or not she was a transsexual. Salvador Dali is reported to have said that she had one of the most perfect faces he had ever seen, which was one of the launchpad quotes for Miss Lear's previous international modelling career. This multi-lingual beauty appears throughout the world on television, always managing top billing, but for years the British have declined her offers to host a European extravaganza.

The Julia Grant story

The BBC in 1994 continued to report on the progress of the transsexual, Julia Grant's life. She became known to the public eye when, in the early eighties, the world saw the commencement of her gender transformation, explicitly followed by a television camera. It was at times a sad tale, punctuated with a life of problems, many of which seemed to have arisen from an abused childhood. In her book, she

honestly confesses the depths of depravity that she felt she
fell to, in order to survive. Not long after her surgery Julia
collapsed and was rushed to hospital. The doctors, not
realising that she was a transsexual and had just undergone
surgery, thought she was miscarrying and damaged her
newly constructed vagina. Julia survived this tragedy and
is now considering a second surgery.

When reviewing the transsexual situation, it would be
blinkered to ignore this documentary, which will
undoubtedly be shown throughout the world. Fortunately,
the camera does not lie, recording the abysmal inhuman
treatment she received from one of the world's so called,
leading experts in the field. In spite of this, she seems to
hang on to some kind of self respect, viewing life how it
really is for her, a struggle to survive in the face of a system
that legally denigrates her. When considering if she would
make the same choices again, it becomes obvious that she
felt there could have been no other route than the one she
fought for.

Few people would be brave enough to expose their inner
feelings this way and she is a public example of why
humanity should be more careful when dealing with other
people's property -their lives.

First and second generation primary transsexuals are
now coming through their life's journeys as doctors,
lawyers, business people and writers, proving to society
what an unthreatening, additional bonus to humankind
they can be. Around the world networks of previously
gender dysphoric ex-patients help support those who may
be only just entering into the vortex of an unregulated
existence as their whole selves.

The importance of social networks
In the unexpected event of a personal relationship disaster,
the extended family quite often is there to help pick up the
pieces and put them together again. When Abervan in
Wales suffered a coal slag-heap slide in the sixties, killing
innocent schoolchildren, then it was the community at

large that formed support networks. So, why is it, when one transsexual comes across another one in the supermarket checkout queue, they both hide behind the baked beans pretending to be heterosexual shelf fillers?

The answer can be easily understood when we look at the way some Jews denied their Yiddish roots under interrogation, during the second world war. It is a case of survival amongst a hostile force. This must stop, as the only real way for the transsexual minority to persuade the heterosexual majority that they are not going to put up with any more trannie-bashing, is to net-work.

The introduction of a "Trannie Pride day" or a "Date a Trannie week" may not at the moment be the answer, but it is an option well worth considering. The old images of men in wigs gathering in church halls with a visiting psychiatrist has to be squashed. A proliferation of "Glad to be a Trannie" groups needs to be formed in order to help transsexuals fight against apathy, which proves to be their own worst enemy.

Many support groups of families and friends of those who have undergone the transsexual experience, have sprung up all over the world. These groups help those involved to cope with their own feelings and the way in which they can deal with the immediately gender dysphoric. Such associations offer positive future life plans for the family and friends to consider adopting towards the transsexual. Certainly a policy of professionally assisted integration with the family is being sympathetically pursued in Holland now, leaving the Dutch once again with the prize for humanity.

We became aware during the research for the book, talking to Petra Klene of the Humanitas organisation in Holland that the Dutch model, although far from being perfect, was in fact the most complete and humane treatment that transsexuals could receive. Due to their social order and liberal attitudes towards sex, many of the Dutch have a positive outlook towards sexual problems of any kind.

Mermaids
This is an organisation which is a family support group for children with gender identity issues that made its conference debut at the 1996 Gendy's Conference at Manchester University. The pressure that a group like this has been able to exert now encourages clinicians in treating gender dysphoric children, adolescents and families. One of the founders who spoke also talked about the profound experience of having support from other people to help her gender dysphoric child.

Small magazines and leaflets
These are often circulated on a small private basis or even funded from different charitable sources. They are immensely useful to the trans-community in helping people to share their experiences. Advertisements for accommodation, jobs, support networks and many of the basic necessities of life are listed and discussed. People who may not feel comfortable in approaching the trans-community can have a point of contact and listing of resources.

Much talk has been raised about the necessity for gender identity clinics and private practices to supply leaflets which describe the kind of treatment they can offer. The majority of pre-surgical transsexuals have never seen the results of the kind of operations they may undergo. It is imperative for any clinician to ensure that open channels of communication are maintained via plainly written material.

Careers
To give up everything for an ideal is not uncommon as many people decide quite suddenly, for one reason or another, to change their lives out of all recognition. To consider the event of a person's all possessing transsexuality as free choice is not to understand it at all. For those whose lives are taken over by this experience, there is no other option but to try and realign their bodies

with what they believe is their real self; nothing, but nothing is too high a price to pay to try to find some relief from their state of perceived hell.

A career is a way of earning a living to pay the bills. Its prestige as an entity within itself should not really count if it is part of a life that is making a person unhappy. However, life is never so simple. Many secondary transsexuals have abandoned quite dazzling careers to pursue their quests to be themselves. In an ideal world this should not be necessary, but it often is. A husband and father of two, who suddenly wants to be called "Suzy" may not always rely upon the good side of human nature from his former spouse. The transsexual may flee the life they were living, job and all.

A mother of three who may feel she is really a "Richard" may perhaps have difficulty changing her role from the mother to that of a second father. In such complicated metamorphosis's, not everyone can accommodate the new person the transsexual is becoming and that could well include their boss.

Back in the seventies and beyond, complisexuals were encouraged to cut any ties with a life they may have previously led, abandoning everything that went before. These days some people manage, not only to keep the life they have led before, but also their jobs. Our studies have shown that this can often be to their disadvantage, giving them the public image, to many, as a local curiosity. Those who have started anew are generally able to integrate much easier into society, as few people, if any, will know their backgrounds. This is not to say that picking up the pieces of a broken life is necessarily negative, as there are many complisexuals who have gone on to build very successful second careers too.

Some transsexuals have remained in their pre-change environment, held their ground and won through and now days this is more possible. This course has been a particularly hard road to follow and those who have walked it will tell of its benefits and its drawbacks.

With primary transsexuals, the matter of career can sometimes be easier, in so far as many changed their lives so young that they did not have a lot of history to lose. Some go on to build the lives and careers they would have wanted for themselves, although quite naturally, a certain number never become accustomed to the life they fought so hard for. The trauma of their condition can often leave some dysfunctioning in the work place.

Not everyone can become a pop star like Amanda Lear, a model like Caroline Cossey or an intellectual such as Jan Morris. Life is tough and the workplace can be a particularly difficult area for transsexuals. The help of sympathetic family and friends is usually the biggest ally that anyone in this position can have.

Relationships

Relationships are another minefield where transsexuals have difficulty finding their feet. When to tell a potential partner or date, or whether to tell them at all? These are issues that make life very difficult when complisexuals have to deal with them alone, without support, in total isolation and secrecy. In a world conforming to stereotypes of male and female and expectations of breeding, the complisexual can either be rejected as a freak, unable to bear or produce children, or dated simply because they are a curiosity.

We have also come across transsexuals in relationships that have been very successful and satisfying for them. These seem to be the ones who have come to terms with their condition and shared some of that knowledge of the experience with their partners. Living The Secret (purposely not disclosing) appeared to be a guaranteed time bomb that was a problem just waiting to happen and when the Secret came out the partner was often very unhappy that they had not been confided in.

Even some "friends" may reject the transsexual when finding out that the person they originally befriended was born of a different biological sex. It seems that for those people all the good things about the transsexual that led to a friendship being formed in the first place just disappear after the discovery of the condition. This can lead to a very stressful way of life, not knowing if you are going to be found out and if you are, if you are going to be rejected. It is little wonder then that some transsexuals are loathe to form close relationships for fear of being hurt, preferring to live sheltered and lonely lives, a very sad state of affairs that society allows this to happen.

Childlessness

One of the tormenting issues faced by primary complisexuals is their inability to have children. This is an issue often so painful that no fertile person could begin to imagine the uncontrollable longings that are coupled with a sense of barrenness. Add to this the fact that, in some countries, transsexuals are not even allowed to adopt or foster children in their new identity, and it is clear just how horrendously unfair life can be for the complisexual who wishes to be a parent. Of course now, in some countries it is indeed possible for transsexual people to become parents, although this is quite rare. The psychological disturbances that can develop in long-term gender dysphoric people who are unable to become parents we have identified as a condition we have called Chronic Childlessness Syndrome (pertaining to gender dysphoria).

When Tracie, at thirty-two years of age, on the brink of suicide, took this problem to a professional counsellor, she was mortified by the response that met her. The counsellor could not see any problem. As far as she was concerned, Tracie had given up the right to ever be a parent, of any kind, upon the eve of her gender reaffirment surgery.

The counsellor also did not think it was a good idea that any transsexual should be around children. She believed that a possible transference of behavioural patterns might take place from the adult to the child, causing gender dysphoria in the child. Sad to say, this counsellor still works in London for the British National Health system. Such dangerous practitioners quite easily gain their qualifications in counselling, destroying much of the good work carried out by those who are genuinely empathetic and understanding.

We would like to stress that, like homosexuality, transsexuality is NOT catching. Neither is it something which can be passed on to children or corrupt them. Dr. Richard Green, Professor of psychiatry at London's Charing Cross Hospital has published reports to this effect, in which the children of homosexuals had no higher incidence of being homosexual themselves than the children of heterosexuals. In fact, most homosexual people are born of heterosexuals.

In his speech at the GENDY'S Conference in Manchester, 1994, he said that children were far more accepting of both homosexuality and transsexuality than many adults around them. Transsexuals are, above all, people, just like you and I, some good, some bad, all with their own hang-ups, confusions, successes and failures. To deny them the right to be parents in their new identity is most unjustified, after all there are many heterosexual people who make terrible parents and subject their children to horrifying abuse. Surely it is better for a child to be brought up in a loving and caring environment, regardless of the parent's gender, sex or sexuality.

Children
With secondary complisexuals who may have children whom they mothered or fathered before their metamorphosis into their new gender role, they often risk losing their children if the spouse has no compassion or understanding of the transsexual condition. We met a couple of people in our research whose spouses had rejected them totally, to the point of hatred and had told the children that their "mother" or "father" was dead. These two transsexuals have never seen their offspring since their change-over, one of which was seven years ago, the other twelve years.

Prostitution and transsexuality

The point at which a young, teenage person may coherently incorporate their transsexualism into their life plan may be a time when childhood fades and the cruel realities of shaping their own lives present them with a very narrow set of alternatives. Idealistically, the nuclear family, having been a childhood support mechanism, would extend its protective barriers to those who dysfunction in society, for whatever reasons. Life however, is not such things as dreams are made of.

The trauma experienced when an individual discovers their own transsexualism, is to say, the very least, cataclysmic. Survival and gender re-dress become the primary targets, ninety-nine per cent of the time to the detriment of career, family relationships, background or a previously law abiding concept of the world at large. A period of several years of disorientation may take place from the beginning of treatment until the individuals eventually find their feet in their new identity. Should the establishment and the family prove to be supportive prior to and during the transitionary period of gender reaffirment, then all well and good, but for many transsexuals this is not the case. Many primary transsexuals, alienated from their roots and unaided by society, turn to a career in prostitution, usually though not always through necessity rather than choice.

The facts of life for many transsexuals, who cannot afford their necessary treatment, are that medical assistance is very expensive. Prostitution provides the desperately needed funds, whilst not questioning the transsexual's apparent dysfunctional existence, but sometimes exalting it. There is a huge market where men and even women will pay handsomely for encounters of the exploratory kind, beyond what may be available in their local brothels.

Prefemisexuals especially are sought after, endlessly by men, searching for the "woman with a prick", and certainly the trannie prostitutes we know and met are busy every single day. As soon as they have saved enough money for all their surgery, they then, post-operatively, become less of a fascination to these men. However there is no shortage of other prefemisexuals desperate for the money for their operations, to take their place. Once having got into prostitution and living on the edge of life, it can be very difficult for complisexuals to then go on into mainstream society and pursue a "straight" career, if that is what they would like to do. It is difficult enough for a biological female prostitute to do this, let alone the transsexual, who has so much prejudice and hostility to cope with too, hence many of them continue in this career whether it is what they really want or not. The converse of this is that some secondary transsexuals go into prostitution after having had a previously "straight" career, which they have been unable to go back into.

We also encountered some mascusexuals from America who were making a living as rent boys and a man from Japan who was listed and hired out by his agency as a mascusexual.

Dr. Susan Carr of Scotland has raised the heady question as to whether those who are involved in the sex industry should legitimately be considered to go through the systems that deal with gender dysphoria. Her premise is that perhaps their profession alone should not preclude them from the treatment they may so desperately need and in fact that those who are happy in their work as prostitutes should be considered self-supporting financially.

Transsexuals in prison

Maxine Peterson of Canada has made an international study of the rights of transsexuals in prison to medical, psychological and humane treatment. The results demonstrated that it was extremely hard for any transsexual who found themselves caught up in the penal system. Medication and treatment could be withdrawn or withheld without reasons needing to be given by the authorities.

Naturally, from country to country and culture to culture

the issues surrounding the treatment of transsexual offenders differ, but one thing was obvious – that transsexuals were almost always abused within prisons or other corrective establishments. Rape, beatings, murder and constant mental abuse were common in every country, not only by other prisoners, but also by the guards themselves.

It is extremely difficult for many transsexuals to survive oppressive inhumane regimes and often these people become socio-economic victims forced into crime. This is indicative of the way many cultures actually see transsexualism itself – as a moral and legal crime.

A controversial case came to light recently in Leeds Prison in England when a twice convicted murderer declared that he believed he was transsexual and demanded treatment. An open debate commenced as to the validity of funding treatment for transsexualism when it concerns a life-term prisoner who already costs the government a great deal of money. It seems that there were private discussions between doctors and the Home Office to set up a special unit for transsexuals, but unfortunately the hard-line Michael Howard took over as minister in charge. The outcome of this situation is still awaited as the balance between the humanitarian treatment of prisoners and cost cutting continues to rock back and forth.

Chapter Six

Politics and the Law

In March 1954 Peter Wildeblood was sentenced to eighteen months in a British prison for homosexual offences. The "Montagu case" was the subject of considerable public controversy. It was largely responsible for the government's decision to set up a committee to enquire into the whole question of homosexuality relating to the law. Forty years later in the 1990s the British government, along with many other regimes, are still using discriminatory laws against minority sexualities.

Many years after the ignorance of Queen Victoria, who refused to outlaw lesbianism because she did not believe there could ever be such a thing, ludicrous gaggles of politicians still have very little concept of what a lesbian or homosexual is, never mind a transsexual. Similar incongruities permit the majority of the world's heterosexual rule books to be used with malice against the transsexual population. Taking all this confusion into account, is it any wonder that a considerable amount of people are not even sure what a transsexual is, quite apart from which laws apply to them and how?

In early cases of transsexualism, where the transformation of one biological sex to a cosmetically constructed opposite sex had taken place, a change to the person's birth certificate was allowed. One of the first recorded cases was in Switzerland in 1945. Genuine cases of hermaphroditism, where people have grown up realising they were designated the wrong sex at birth, have generally had no problems in getting their birth sex identity changed, giving them the full protection of the law.

Complisexuals, although having been assisted by society to redefine themselves are today facing the agonising position of not having the law's protection. Governments continue to discriminate on the basis that a historical document (birth certificate) may not be altered. The standard chromosome test, having now been proved to be not so reliable or simple as once thought, remains the legal Damocles sword with which heterosexuality denies transsexuals their basic human rights.

There is little general awareness of the presence of complisexuals in society, because most of them cannot be detected as being anything other than what they appear. For these people a genetic accident or developmental result should not be the basis of their legal denigration. Surely many people died fighting a war trying to stop Hitler doing that sort of thing. Or is a new kind of eugenics just around the corner?

The rights of the individual to define the self must be at the very fundaments of any society, otherwise we have a dictatorship, no matter what political system you wish to define it as. To deliberately exclude a sector of society from the human rights' stature, is not only cruel, it is the very reason sanctions were used against South Africa and guns against Saddam Hussein. Having considered this, we come full circle, in considering if the transsexual existence is a threat to society. Whose society? What society? In what way? Can evidence be produced to substantiate such a claim? Who will decide the validity of that evidence?

The law is a process that is frequently being misused by official political powers who are always looking for scapegoat minorities. Transsexuals are easily identified as the potential prey of a political witch hunt and are forced to live in fear of discovery. Most transsexuals do not want to test the prejudicial ignorance of heterosexual insecurities, but just wish to be left in peace. For these very reasons, many live under false identities, leaving them with little rights or pensions. In all reality the young woman living next door to you could be transsexual, or the man from whom you buy your bread. However, they will keep their secret silent, for fear that their lives could be torn apart by intrusive officialdom(the men in grey suits, who watch our every move).

The legal rights of transsexuals must be reviewed, omitting prejudicial discrimination on the basis that a person is or may develop into a transsexual. These basic human rights must move in line globally with the legal privileges given to heterosexuals and some homosexuals. That is not to say that many people are not sympathetic to this cause and also help, love and assist transsexuals in their difficulties.

April Ashley

The case of *"Corbett versus Corbett"* in 1970 set a very nasty and prejudicial legal precedent in England. The judge, who was also a physician declared April Ashley to legally be a man, therefore annulling her marriage to her husband who was also a member of the peerage. During the divorce case Miss Ashley was not awarded property rights or a settlement, due to the fact that, in the eyes of the law, she had never been her husband's spouse. It was acknowledged that April was fully capable of a sexual relationship, having undergone surgery.

Ironically the husband had reportedly known his wife was transsexual before they had married, but nevertheless, the judge ruled the annulment in his favour. The husband, Lord Rowallan kept all the money, all the property and his old school tie, whilst April only gained an opportunity to improve on her celebrity status. In her autobiography, "Odyssey", she tells of the triumphs and tribulations of her colourful life. Far from ending up embittered, she fled to her ex-husband's bedside, in 1993 when she heard he was ill. Still as demure as ever, Miss Ashley now lives on the west coast of America and says how she still loves Britain, but finds it so backward when it comes to sex. Her heart, she says, will always be British, but the government had condemned her to being a freak in exile.

The medical profession

The medical fraternity does not always agree on a number of scientific theories, until proven many times over. Rarely has there been such a medical anomaly that has depended so much upon listening to the voice of the patient, a concept which the elite patriarchy of medicine finds rather disempowering. As a matter of human rights, psychiatrists, endocrinologists, geneticists and surgeons should be putting before the law-makers the real facts about the variations in human sexuality, sex and gender. Only by the medical fraternity backing transsexuals will they be able to claim their equality in law. Human rights groups such as Amnesty International are preoccupied with a war-torn world where genocide and tyrannical abuse are their main concerns, and it will be a long time before they get around to fighting an issue like transsexualism.

Toilets

The question of which public toilet a pre-operative transsexual should legally be entitled to use is a delicate point. Idealistically, if a person is under treatment for gender dysphoria and is living as a member of their opposite biological sex, then they should be allowed to use the toilet designated as such. However, not all transsexuals pass undetected in their new gender and it is understandable that some members of the public may be distressed to perceive that a person of the opposite sex is intruding in the wrong toilet.

Insurance

Many insurance companies and health authorities have tried to wheedle their way out of paying for any treatment, which has been part of a person's gender dysphoria. During gender reassignment, some surgeons have had to design the operations within the constraints of the small print of medical insurance. Sometimes these operations have not been in the best interests of the client, but the only way in which they were able to have surgery at all. Even on the matter of life, car or home insurance the policy may be made null and void by the company should they find out the holder is transsexual and has not declared it.

In Portugal it was illegal to even carry out gender reaffirment surgery until the summer of 1995. Up until then, both the patient and the surgeon involved would have been put in prison. In Sweden the government has to give its approval for such an operation to take place. What if it disagrees? Where is the patient left then? By what divine authority do such fascists think they have the right to define life?

In Spain the law is constantly being changed and different courts are renowned for interpreting it in different ways. What purpose such an inconsistency serves has been very hard for us to define, no matter how many people we spoke to from Spain.

In New Zealand and Australia it is already possible for transsexuals to have their birth certificates changed after surgery, giving a complisexual the full civil rights in their new gender. The Antipodes, not having a history of Overlords, probably have a slicker and more flexible legal system that is not encumbered by a feudal past. Also, in some Islamic societies such as Egypt and Turkey, there is a reported proliferation of transsexuals, who can often have their birth certificates amended without any fuss at all.

One mascusexual who constantly travels between two countries in Europe finds himself in a hilarious predicament. On one side of the border he is male and on the other side of the border he is female, even though his passport says male. He jokingly proclaims that he has changed his sex more times than any one in the world.

Children and the law

In some countries, there is nothing written in the law that prevents transsexuals from adopting children, but when it comes to reality, they are turned down. Sadly, some law systems prevent transsexuals from having contact with children whom they may have previously parented. A directive from Strasbourg in February 1994 told the member states of the EEC that homosexuals should be allowed to be marry and adopt children. The directive is not being implemented in many countries, so what chances do transsexuals have, when they are a much smaller minority?

A generation of primary complisexuals has produced those who have lived no other adult life, possibly having a partner and children, for whom they do not want any kind of trauma. Society still has many problems in coming to terms with the gay family, contrary to legal documentation. The transsexual family is a concept that the majority of the public have not even, as yet imagined.

Equality in England?

In England, it is reported that the Baroness Miller of Hendon made the following statement on the 14th July 1995:

"The government's position is clear. We oppose unjustified discrimination against any person on grounds of their sex, race, colour, ethnic origin or for any other reason, irrespective of where that discrimination occurs. Everyone is entitled to equal treatment and, at work, to be assessed on merit against objective criteria, not on the basis of prejudice and stereo-typing....unjustified discrimination is morally unacceptable and economically inefficient."

When we wrote to the Ministry of Defence enquiring about the exclusion of non heterosexuals from employment in the Armed Forces, we received a letter from Squadron leader J. A. Small, BA, RAF, SP, Pol 2C1. This letter was signed Jennifer, but gave no indication of what sex the author was. It told us that an exclusion policy could be activated under UK domestic law and that the EC equal treatment directive did not apply as the Armed Forces was a special case. However we have heard of transsexuals in countries other than Britain such as Holland being admitted to the Armed Forces.

Private Member's Bill

On 2nd February 1996 a private Members Bill for the civil rights for transsexuals was presented to the British House of Commons. The Bill's second reading was brought by Alex Carlile, QC, MP, himself a lawyer and supported by Lynne Jones, MP. Prior to the debate, many MP's promised to look into the situation. However, the Right Honourable Sir John Wheeler, JP, DL, MP warned one of the campaigners in a letter that many controversial bills are opposed by a counter lobby and do not make sufficient progress. He himself was unable to be anything but aloof from the process, because he was a minister and would not get involved unless required to give a government view (he failed to say what the government view was).

Not surprisingly then, the Bill was talked out after a period of thirty five minutes and was therefore not successful in getting through the House. It was stated that although the government takes these issues seriously, it would not support this Bill, being unconvinced that it effectively resolves the birth certificate issue.

Amongst the Bill's supporters were Roger Sims (Conservative), Kevin Barron (Labour spokesperson) and Edwina Currie (Conservative) who all spoke in favour of the legislation. John Horam (Parliamentary Under Secretary of State for Health) responded for the government. Private Member's Bills often have little chance of becoming law and many receive no discussion at all. It was therefore thought by supporters of the Press for Change movement (see Groups and Organisations at the end of this chapter), that a discussion time of thirty five minutes was a most positive step forward, bringing some of the relevant issues into high public profile. There were reports that it was one of the most effective lobbying campaigns seen in the House for twenty-five years. However, a system set up by Oliver Cromwell failed to serve the needs of transsexuals in 1996.

Campaigning continued by Lynne Jones, MP, to push for

civil rights for transsexuals by moving onto a procedure of measuring the support amongst MP's. The organisation, Press for Change continued to lobby and set up test cases to go to court for a wide range of civil right's issues concerning marriage, change of birth certificate, adoption, rights to privacy and to have treatment paid for on the British National Health System.

Conservative trannies

To the surprise of many, Miss Christine Burns, a forty two year old computer consultant came out as a transsexual at the September 1995 Conservative Party Conference in England. She turned out to be the secretary of her local Conservative Party branch and Chair of the women's constituency supper club.

It seems that in the very heartland of a political system that denies transsexuals their human rights are transsexuals themselves. She had been active for years, secretly campaigning for transsexual rights, but only felt safe as public opinion shifted to come out amongst her fellow party members. Christine reported that she had received nothing but support from her colleagues and remains the secretary and Vice-Chair of the branch.

Marriage

Marriage is a contentious issue that puts transsexuals in a non status position, leaving them open to exploitation in their relationships. A recent case in England drove a transsexual to attempt suicide when her disgruntled husband threatened her with the newspapers if she did not give him everything he wanted in their divorce case. Unable to take the stress of the Sunday newspapers, she packed a bag, leaving her home, business and friends behind. The fear of the gutter press and harassment from unjust laws lost her everything she had worked for all her life. For her, the abandonment of her former life was her only escape from public humiliation.

A right to work

We heard of a case in England where a mascusexual school teacher going through his change was suspended from his job. When he agreed to call himself by his previous female name he was allowed back to work. However, when he turned up for work dressed as a man, sporting a full beard and a deep voice, the school authorities retired him on a full pension. Of course, he was as pleased as punch, but the authority, through their stupidity, lost a good teacher and a lot of money.

The main theme of Steven Whittles' address, at the Harry Benjamin Conference 1995, was the right to employment. Now, as the world begins to realise that transsexualism is a medical condition, then protection in the workplace must be assured. There have been many exploitations of the current situation in law, where employers have dismissed people for being transsexual. The loophole seems to have emerged because the laws have referred specifically to male, female and sometimes homosexuals but not to transsexuals. Perhaps in some cultures these references were accidentally left out but in others it was no doubt deliberate.

It is not so much the transsexualism that is disabling, but some people's uneducated attitude towards it. To say that transsexuals were the only ones that were discriminated against in the work place, would be wrong as it happens to ethnic minorities, mentally and physically disabled people, religious denominations, transgenderists, homosexuals and women.

Happily, progress is being made in this area, even thought it is a slow process. Georgina Beyer, who used to work as a prostitute, stripper and actor became New Zealand's first transsexual mayor in the Carterton District Council, a small rural community. Before standing for office, she had been a popular councillor for the district and despite an apparent malicious smear campaign by her critics she earned her victory with 1108 votes.

Cornwall County Council

In England, a profound breakthrough was made in early 1996, as a transsexual won a case in the European Court of Justice against their ex-employer, Cornwall County Council. In this employment discrimination case of *P* v *S* and Cornwall County Council, the Attorney-General's recommendation to the European Court of Justice was that the European Council Directive on the principle of equal treatment for men and women should be held to cover transsexuals.

The transsexual, who had been employed by Cornwall County Council, had lost their job after informing their employers that they were go undergo treatment for gender dysphoria. The case that was presented ruled that had that person not been treated for gender dysphoria and had remained in their original biological gender, they would have still been employed by the council. This was a monumental European Court decision to change the law to prevent sex discrimination against transsexuals at work and hopefully is a pattern that will filter throughout the rest of the world. One day perhaps governments will realise it is better to have a person in full employment paying tax than to have them living off the state.

Forming transsexual spaces

Daphne Spain, an associate professor of urban and environmental planning, in her book "Gendered Spaces", examined the sociological implications of women's access to knowledge by infiltrating the spaces of their oppressors. Parallels can be drawn here with the fight that lies ahead for transsexual rights. Those now hiding behind the mask of heterosexuality in silence cannot help the cause if they refuse to be identified. What was once the desire simply to lead an ordinary life no longer seems possible, because the mere fact of being transsexual legally excludes a person from an egalitarian society. Transsexuals are now going to have to try and create their own spaces in society.

Women and ethnic minorities have had to fight to

empower themselves against a white, patriarchal, bigoted, racist, sexist society. The only way out of oppression for transsexuals is to recognise their differences and quantify them as an identity. There should be no public space where a transsexual has not been known. Infiltration, integration and a refusal to be excluded, on the basis of gender alone, must be aligned with a new sense of transsexual pride.

Time for Change

Ultimately the laws of any culture are a maze of non laws and jargon that can only ever be interpreted by the experts. There is little doubt that there is a need for clarification in law throughout the world. At the moment the ludicrous state of confusion that exists, not only disadvantages the transsexuals themselves, but their families, friends and the very people who have to interpret the legal inexactitudes.

Things are now changing. There is a new undercurrent arising from those who have undergone gender re-affirment, unwilling to put up with an inferior status anymore. Like any other subculture, eventually people learn to link up, share ideas, compare notes and begin to demand their civil and human rights. Now, since transsexuals have learned to network, by modelling other minorities' fights for freedom, things have begun to happen.

Trannies on the internet are something else. It seems that throughout the world they are vibrantly exchanging ideas, resources and knowledge. In cyberspace a new transsexual community is forging and perpetually re-inventing itself. Deep in Tran-Com where anyone can be anything with only a name to identify one's sex, sexuality and gender even the non transsexual can dip their toe into the gender fluid adventure.

Lawyers throughout the world are continuously confronting the legal systems with cases of individuals, who are demanding their rights of gender, sexuality and sex. In every country there may be lawyers who are sympathetic to the plight of transsexuals and their names may be obtained from self-help groups. High profile, public, political activists like Phyllis Randolph-Frye, the American lawyer, are beginning to bang on the door of Congress, refusing to go away. Europe sits in a position of uncomfortableness, as the transsexual community relentlessly refuses to accept the unsatisfactory decision the EEC court passed upon human rights, of the Caroline Cossey case. Letters are being written to politicians, petitions signed, trade unions lobbied and most effectively, transsexuals are personally presenting themselves to the law-makers.

Transsexuals, like anyone else, want to be kind and patient, finding squabbles over differences in sex, tedious, but their resistance to oppression is now rising forcefully around the world. The Gays have taken California, the Blacks Atlanta, the Jews Golders Green and if no kind of political and legal equality is forthcoming soon, then the sleeping bigots of Suburbia should begin to lock their doors twice – or maybe even three times.

World-wide, people like Steven Whittle, Professor Richard Green, Professor Swartz, Leah Schaefer, Professor Gooren, Mark Rees, Caroline Cossey, Frau Auchstein, Dr. Russell Reid, we, the authors and tens of thousands of others have been and are fighting to change the laws. It is and will be, a continuous process and those that should always be at the front of the fight must be the transsexuals themselves. WHATEVER IT TAKES!

Transsexuality, Homosexuality and Transgenderism

There is the danger that those who are not transsexual, but are trying to align themselves, may unintentionally, in their own separate gender journey, muddy the waters of the transsexual issues. Undoubtedly, the issues of the transgenderist are only partly those of the complisexual; but in adopting an elitist stance, is complisexuality guilty of the very discrimination which they are fighting against?

A short-cut method of tapping into an already existing, consolidated political power is to align the transsexual's fight for equality alongside the gay and lesbian movement. The gay and lesbian community, under their umbrella of caring radicalism, has, over time, sheltered the fate of many a politically disadvantaged individual. For the first time in England, the 1996 Gay Pride March was entitled "Lesbian, Gay, Bisexual and Transgender March". We welcome this as an opportunity for transsexuals and transgendered people to become visible and claim their rights. However, we also acknowledge the other side of the coin in that by aligning transsexualism with homosexuality, is that then playing into the hands of heterosexual paranoia?

Transsexualism has succeeded in being taken out of the American compendium of mental disorders D.S.M.4 (Diagnostic and Statistic Manual of Mental Disorders – published by the American Psychiatric Association), declaring that it is neither a heterosexual disorientation nor a homosexual derivative. Can hard-core transsexuals once again allow themselves to be misclassified, regardless of their own sexual orientation, unless it is defensively included amongst a wide spectrum of minorities, such as gays?

This may be the best option for now until such a time when we understand more about the origins of the condition. By accepting this comprise as a best temporary haven from present discrimination should in no way be interpreted as a slur upon the hospitality of gays. However, as transsexual survival grows, it would prefer not to share a statistical analysis with any other sexuality, sex or gender.

There are many femisexuals who never consider taking a male lover after their treatments, immediately becoming translesbians. In London, in the Summer of '95, at the Chelsea registry office, the first lesbian wedding took place through a legal loophole. One of the brides was a post operative transsexual who used to a merchant seaman. Both brides arrived in full wedding dress regalia, in a chauffeur-driven limousine to an onslaught of press and public interest. Their honeymoon was described as a quiet period where they would both to be getting to know Mrs and Mrs Scott-Dixon.

The well-known complisexual writer, Kate Bornstein found herself waking up one morning faced with her partner, who had discovered s/he was a premascusexual. We believe the two of them had difficulty in defining the configurations in this relationship, until such a time as they acquainted themselves with the strangest of all facts, that they are both human beings.

During our research we met one femisexual who, pre-operatively had become involved with another pre-femisexual. The former has had gender re-affirment and continues in her relationship with the latter, who will be undergoing gender re-affirment in the future.

A woman from Holland told us of her first child who grew up to become a homosexual male and of her daughter who had a sex reaffirment procedure, also to end up as a homosexual male (transhomosexual).

The emergence of translesbianism and transhomo-sexuality frightens the pants off heterosexuals even more so than the emergence of transsexuality itself. By eventually gaining recognition for the different varieties of transsexuals, those sub-groups may be alienated even more, because they are even smaller minorities. A transsex-educational programme to desensitise the world's concept of heterosexual superiority would be very useful here!

Religion

The major religions now encompassing the world are patriarchally based, worshipping the almighty phallus, belittling womanhood and minority sexualities into an inferior position. It is still an offence to be homosexual in many cultures, punishing the participant by all sorts of barbaric methods, including execution. In the name of a godhead, many wars have been fought and disputes brought onto peacefully coexisting neighbours, who in the past may have lived in a climate of tolerance.

Here it would be political suicide for us to ignore the fact that many wars have also been waged on behalf of a matriarchal deity too. Religion has, throughout history, been the most effective regulator of social, and sexual behaviour, using fear or guilt as its tools of confinement. Behind every philosophy of life lies a politically self motivated, power seeking group or individual, genuflecting their own ego.

Many workers within the Christian church show profound understanding and sympathy towards transsexuals, but it must be said, not all. The church has no coherent policy dealing with the "unclassifiable mutilation of such unfortunates" (the way some churches view transsexuals), generally ignoring their existence. The theological bodies concerned with formulating human ethics prefer to forget transsexuality altogether and hope it will go away. However, considering the Vatican's practice of castrating male singers, so they might sing comfortably in the higher melodic register, a procedure carried out in Rome until this century, maybe the cardinals are wise to stay silent.

Many humane and socially aware priests are quite happy to bless the unions of transsexuals in their churches, even though they might not be able to legally marry them to potential partners. For those transsexuals who wish to become post-operatively homosexual, it is quite legal for a couple both to turn up in bridal dresses or both with moustaches and sideburns, adding to Rome's confusion.

Some religions, over time have offered up the image of the ultimate creation bearing both physical male and female characteristics, to be worshipped as a deity. This cultural engulfment of male strength and female nurturing not only has nothing to do with the rare incidence of hermaphroditism in humans, but also bears absolutely no relation to transsexualism. A culture that worships such iconology is surely exhibiting a social comment on its peaceful cross alignment of its sexes and not the recognition of a person who is at war with their own body.

In Asia, the Tamils had cast a one piece statue in bronze of a god, two whole centuries before Donatello's accomplishments. This god encompassed the twin natures of male and female in perfect harmony and unison. Ironically, the West has the nerve to call this third world country backward. The image of the phallus would be repugnant to any prefemisexual, whilst the breast enlargement of womanhood might prove extremely embarrassing to a premascusexual, should anyone try to connect these images with transsexualism.

Religious based structures, built around the rigid heterosexual role models, have trouble recognising transsexualism at all. They find the very essence of sexual differences to be a threat of anarchy. Such cults, based around the worship of the power of the almighty phallus are not only afraid of transsexual notions, but also display a paranoia about homosexuality.

Native Americans allow social spaces for those warriors absent of manhood (the winyanktehca). They become shamans and healers, being regarded as having a hotline to the gods. Respect is afforded to them in accordance with their supposed divine wisdom.

The xanith (eunuch) of Oman is not allowed to wear male attire, but parades in colours which are a contrast to the traditional, white, male dress. They are accepted, moving freely amongst women, wearing make-up and heavy perfume. A status of neither male nor female sets them apart from the normal rigidity of the culture's sexual structures.

The hijras of India have their penis, scrotums and testicles removed in an attempt to become holy. Should they survive without bleeding to death then they are feared and revered as initiators at ceremonies, masquerading as female but claiming a neuter status. The Pakistani version of this is called the kushra.

The acaults of Burma, instilled with cross-sex, non-conformist behaviour are considered to be possessed by a spirit. They are not held in any way responsible for their position, as they perform dances at celebrations with all members of the Buddhist believers. No attempt is made to disguise their lack of masculinity.

It seems, throughout the world, that an accommodation of the less rigidly gendered may, in the absence of gender realignment treatment, have occurred spiritually. Who is to say that the West has got it right and transsexualism is the answer? Obviously one thing is for sure, when it comes to the respect for each and every human being's rights to make their own free choices, they presently have a long way to go.

Transsexualism and Feminism

This is a book in itself, however we will attempt to summarise some of the issues concerning transsexualism and feminism, or rather certain factions of feminism, being that the word itself is merely an umbrella for many different ways of thinking, each calling themselves feminism.

In the nineties, the word itself is deemed by some women to be outdated, due to the fact that we are now living in a supposedly post-feminist era. Well, to this group of people, we have to say that in our opinion, as long as women's salaries are less than men, as long as women continue to be raped by men, patronised, abused and stereotyped into the patriarchal roles that men like us to be kept in, we are nowhere near post anything. As long as a man can screw around as much as he likes and is deemed the cool, acceptable stud and a woman who does the same is deemed negatively as a slut and a whore, we are not post anything. As long as images of women as dutiful wives and mothers, subservient to their husbands are thrust down our throats, we are not post anything. And anyone who believes there is no such thing as the Old Boys Network is not living in the same world as the rest of us.

The Women's Movement began in the sixties and really came to fruition in the early seventies alongside the Gay Liberation Movement. Women in this movement were seen by the rest of society as radical lesbians, rejecting anything associated with femininity. This included burning of their bras, shaving their heads, not wearing skirts nor any make-up. Frightened by what the Women's Movement stood for, patriarchal society portrayed these women as freaks and unnatural. These particular women were the only ones whom the press showed to the rest of the world – the fact that they were only a small section of the movement as a whole was irrelevant. The government wanted to frighten any "normal" women thinking of joining the ranks of the Women's Movement into staying in their subservient position to men

It is true that certain of these women separated into a group of their own, under the banner of lesbian separatists and rejected outright anything remotely male. In some cases this led to rejecting their own fathers, brothers or even sons. However, in the movement there were also women who merely wanted the same equal rights for women as for men. Some were heterosexual, some bisexual and some lesbian. Amidst these two extremes were women with varying degrees of beliefs and political awareness, all grouped together under the heading of feminism. As mentioned earlier, the media only really honed in on the former group and in the seventies the term feminism became synonymous with butch, shaven-headed, man-hating dykes.

The eighties saw the rise of more women up the corporate ladder. Some of these women wore trouser suits and the media accused them of trying to look like men. Other women tended to be glamorous in so far as they wore make-up and fashion wise, shoulder pads and pencil skirts became popular, reinventing the image of the smouldering femme fatale of the forties portrayed on the screen by actresses like Bette Davis and Joan Crawford.

The nineties has seen an economic recession and there now seems to be a split between the religious faction of government, who are calling for a return to good, old-fashioned family values and morality, and youthful media types such as Katie Puckrick of "The Pyjama Party" fame, claiming to be "progressive" post feminists. And, of course there are still those women, who, masquerading under the banner of feminism, discriminate and attack transsexuals' right to exist. One such woman is Janice Raymond, whose vicious, uneducated and ill-informed book, "The Transsexual Empire" attacks, in particular, femisexuals.

Ms Raymond accuses femisexuals of raping women's bodies by trying to assimilate them and in her view, transsexual lesbian feminists go one step further by raping women's minds and spirits. She makes constant references to femisexuals as men and mascusexuals as women.

Although the book is mainly an attack on femisexuals whom she sees as castrated men trying to infiltrate women's spaces, she does briefly mention mascusexuals. She accuses them of being merely tokens to promote the fact that transsexualism is a human problem, rather than a male one, this fact she sees as a deception. In other words, she views transsexualism as men wanting to disempower women, by joining their ranks and the few mascusexuals she met as merely exceptions. She herself had great difficulty in tracking down mascusexuals to interview and therefore came to the conclusion that there were not many at all around.

Even after reading studies from distinguished institutions like the John Hopkins Hospital which specialises in the treatment and research into transsexualism, that the occurrence of mascusexuals is rising and more and more are now coming forward for treatment, Ms Raymond disputes this information, simply because it does not fit in with her own theories. It obviously did not occur to Ms Raymond that the reason she could not find many mascusexuals was that so many of them just integrate themselves in life as men and get on with it, not wishing to come out for fear of public backlash – such as that of Ms Raymond's? Or perhaps when word got out that she was writing the book, they all dived for cover and actively hid themselves until she had gone away.

Ms Raymond declares that femisexuals only WANT to be women, but believes that they never can be. She thinks that because they do not have the history of being a woman or suffering from patriarchal oppression, instead having enjoyed male privileges, they should not be allowed into women-only spaces, as they are still men. In her book, she interviewed only thirteen femisexuals, before coming to her opinions. We can only assume that some of the transsexuals she met were secondary femisexuals, who, perhaps did live a part or a lot of their lives in a male role, fighting against their transsexuality or perhaps not discovering it until much later in life and thereby conforming to the roles of husband or father and yes, maybe previously benefiting in certain ways, from privileges afforded to men in our society.

However, Ms Raymond does not take into account the huge number of primary femisexuals who, granted do not have the history of being female, only of being transsexual, but they certainly do not have the history of being men either. Even though many transsexuals were not able to receive hormonal or other treatment as children, (only now in the nineties has this treatment been available, especially in Holland), many of them were living and dressing as members of their desired sex as teenagers. Ms Raymond completely ignores the suffering and confusion experienced by these people growing up in what they consider to be the wrong body.

We would like to ask Ms Raymond to consider, how she, the woman-centred feminist would feel if she woke up tomorrow in the body of a man? Would she not be highly distressed and want to return her body to its original sex and if so, how would she feel if so-called feminists then accused her of being a man trying to infiltrate their world, even though she herself knew who she was?

Whilst everyone has a right to their own opinion on any subject, we are compelled to say that in our opinion, this a highly dangerous book, with the author being ill-informed and completing lacking in understanding of the transsexual condition. If a book had been written with an attack on any other minority sector of society, it would have been deemed racist or sexist. Ms Raymond's book, however has been praised by some well-known "feminists" such as Gloria Steinem, as a correct and necessary attack on not only the femisexuals themselves, but also the medical world for providing hormonal and surgical treatment, thereby making transsexualism a big money business. But isn't any medical treatment or discovery big money? Whoever eventually finds the cure for cancer or AIDS is going to be a billionaire many times over, but we don't hear Ms Raymond or Ms Steinem complaining about this, but perhaps they do not dare for fear of the masses' condemnation of their views. Transsexuals, however, appear to be a very easy scapegoat for Ms Raymond and her cronies' pent-up anger at the world.

Yet another example of discrimination is the annual Michigan "Womyn's" Music Festival which is only for "Womyn born Womyn". In 1991, Nancy Burkholder, a femisexual, was escorted from the Michigan Womyn's Music Festival by virtue of the fact that she was transsexual, a classic example of sexual discrimination - the very thing that these "feminists" claim to be fighting.

Was Nancy ejected from this event because she was "out" as a transsexual or "known" to be one? Did she not look like a "real woman", and if so, what does a "real woman" look like? The ridiculousness of a situation like this is obvious when one considers that it was rumoured Jerry Hall, the supermodel was refused entry into certain night-clubs in the seventies, because she was thought to be a transsexual. Also, when the vast majority of these radical women's (or should we say separatist) groups, who are quick to discriminate against other women, look and dress like men, then really piper isn't fooling pussy.

Lesbians and Transsexuals

Instead of welcoming a diversity of experience and combining together to fight the real enemy of patriarchy, lesbians have divided into several different groups, taking on several different issues. In the meantime, patriarchal oppression continues to flourish, as the oppressed fight amongst themselves. Lesbians have spent twenty-five years or so trying to educate heterosexual mainstream culture that they are not "freaks" and that the hostility and hatred they experience are in no way justified. Why then, can these extremist groups not apply the compassion, understanding and acceptance which they desire for themselves, to transsexuals? Lack of education seems to be the answer. Perceiving a femisexual as a man is equivalent to seeing a lesbian as a frigid heterosexual, unable to entrap a man because she is so ugly. Only the demolition of such ignorance will free transsexuals from sexual oppression.

So, we have to come to the conclusion that not all women who call themselves "feminist" are actually so. The basic fundaments of the Women's Movement were originally to achieve the same equal rights for women, as afforded to men. Along the way, it seems that this basic philosophy has been hi-jacked by certain groups and individuals and distorted in the name of feminism. Surely we should all be striving for equal rights as human beings, regardless of gender, sexuality, race, creed or class.

Having said all this, we are by no means wishing to alienate any women or feminists who support the transsexual cause. At the end of the day, we hope that as more is known about the subject, the less hostility there will be from certain sectors of society.

Fortunately, something positive came out of the maltreatment of Nancy Burkholder. Transsexual lesbians began to come well and truly out of the closet, forming such groups as Transgender Nation and magazines such as "TransSisters", giving voice and visibility to feminist and lesbian transsexuals. Groups of women, both transsexual and non transsexual now descend upon the MWMF, handing out fliers and holding workshops with the aim of educating women on the subject of transsexualism. Various lesbian groups like the Lesbian Avengers in San Francisco also welcome transsexual members.

Transsexualism: The current medical viewpoint
With kind thanks to Dr. Russell Reid, Consultant Psychiatrist at the Hillingdon Hospital, Uxbridge for allowing us to quote from the above paper. This was produced for the parliamentary forum on transsexualism chaired by Lynn Jones, MP, 2nd edition 1996.

The paper's purpose was to provide an overview of the best practices in providing effective health care for person's with transsexual syndrome. It talks about how transsexualism is a "Gender Identity Disorder in which there is a strong and ongoing cross-gender identification, i.e a desire to be accepted as a member of the opposite sex". Unfortunately it fails to see sex and gender as a fluid continuum, referring to opposite sexes in comparison with the bipolar reproductive model.

A suggestion of strong evidence that transsexualism is the result of a medical condition possibly influenced by environmental factors is made. The paper further goes on to say how a person who finds themselves to be transsexual loses a substantial part of their civil liberties. An explanation is given that the model of treatment is now moving away from being heavily causation based with a greater accent placed upon socio-biological amelioration.

It goes on to support the viewpoint of Professor John Money(USA) that gender identity causation may be "subdivisible into genetic, pre-natal hormonal, postnatal social, and postpubertal hormonal determinants". The concept of nature and nurture working inextricably hand in glove is put forward.

The final quote of the paper is **"Medically, there is no reason why people receiving treatment for transsexualism and who have permanently changed gender role should be given any lesser legal status than that of any other person".** For those in the fight for personal, professional and legal recognition, this paper may be helpful in stating arguments for equality.

GROUPS AND ORGANISATIONS (SEE APPENDIX B FOR FULL LIST)
International Conference on Transgendered Law and Employment Policy

This conference takes place in Houston, Texas, considering all the issues concerning the transsexual and transgenderist in law and the work place. This is not a group of elitists, their aims are to fight for total equality, uncompromisingly and it is certainly one of the most important symposiums held towards the transsexual and transgendered future anywhere in the world.

Press for change

Press for change is a campaigning group set up in the UK to fight for the rights of transsexuals. Its aims are to gain legal recognition for those, who having undergone sex reaffirment treatment, are now in the legal dichotomy of belonging to no particular sex. As a possible pressure group it may be a focal point that all British transsexuals and their friends or relatives could join to try to effect change.

The Harry Benjamin International Gender Dysphoria Association Inc.

This is a non profit making organisation. After his book "The Transsexual Phenomenon", Harry Benjamin became the considered world authority on the subject and today the association exists so that the various disciplines involved in the issues concerning the gender dysphoric might interact. It sends out a periodic newsletter to its members, keeping them up to date in all matters concerning aetiological research, treatment, the law and socially related matters.

The conference, held in September 1995, in Germany, reviewed the published minimum standards of care expected in the field. These are the laid down expectations that clinicians of all disciplines must minimally supply the patient. Information on obtaining a copy of these minimum standards of care may be obtained by writing directly to the association including an envelope and return postage. It must be noted at this stage that not everywhere in the world adheres to these standards, particularly when surgery is recklessly offered without any psychological screening, usually motivated by a fat cheque.

In the USA alone there are now an estimated minimum 100,000 people who have undergone gender reaffirment treatment and since no regulatory body cares to monitor their treatment, then the Harry Benjamin organisation's standards of care have become accepted as the general guidelines.

SEE APPENDIX C – INTERNATIONAL CONFERENCES

Chapter Seven

Personal Stories

TRANSSEXUAL STORIES
Thomas (mascusexual)

I began to feel different from other girls when I was about four or five. It seemed wrong. I thought I was a boy – but where was my penis? Why couldn't I attend the boys' school or join the cubs and scouts? Between the ages of thirteen and seventeen, I attended a single-sex boarding school, but in order to fit in, I found myself conforming to a female role.

From an early age I despised my body. I became a compulsive washer, believing I could wash my femaleness away. On the onset of puberty, my compulsions grew worse. I bottled up strong feelings about being male. For years I couldn't confide in my family. When I did tell my parents, they were sympathetic, but said nothing could be done.

I joined the WRNS, hoping for a masculine life, but in the early sixties there was little equality. After three years I was given a medical discharge. I began to ask doctors about surgery. Eventually, at twenty-five, I was referred for a hysterectomy and a bilateral mastectomy was done years later. In the sixties "transsexualism" was hardly known and it wasn't until the mid seventies that I began taking testosterone and became aware of other female-to-male transsexuals.

The changeover was quick in some respects and in other ways took me years to gain confidence. Twenty years on, there have been great improvements in surgical techniques, although the phalloplasty is often unsatisfactory. No doubt in another twenty years, the operation will be easier.

My life has been complicated, due to my gender

dysphoria and my acute washing problem. I have had long periods being unemployed or registered sick. Life was, and is tough, but in spite of major problems, I feel I do cope and I'm pleased I changed.

Many transsexuals want to swap one stereotypical gender role for the opposite. For me, it is different. I used to have such dreams, but while I had no choice but to live as a woman, I began to think of myself in a "middle sex". Admittedly when I first changed over, I over did the male role, but I discovered it was unnatural, I couldn't write off my past and didn't want to treat women in a chauvinistic way. Now although I live as a man and am accepted as one by family, friends and strangers, I feel more androgynous and want to balance the masculine and feminine within.

In the past, female-to-males were neglected and the professional help hardly existed. It has only been in recent years that my testosterone levels have been monitored and regular blood tests done. Now medics are prepared to listen to us, the experts, which is a healthy sign.

Gender dysphoria is not restricted to one social class, one race or one culture. The way we are treated is determined by the laws and "norms" of the different societies. Britain, in fact lags behind some countries in recognising transsexuals as worthy citizens. Let's hope we will be accepted as humans one day.

Stephen (mascusexual)

It was the school sports day. I was to run in the under ten's twenty five yard dash. We were bundled into two groups, girls on one side, boys on the other – I looked over at the boys and suddenly I couldn't stop crying. I immediately knew for certain what was wrong, why my childhood years had been so miserable. I knew I should be in the boys' race, not over here in the girls' group.

I suppose I eventually stopped crying because I can remember, after that moment, spending evening after evening in the local library, which was situated at the bottom of our street. I was brought up in a northern city, with a northern working class mentality surrounding every aspect of my existence. The library was my escape route. Books, as such were not allowed at home, they only had any value if they were children's science or fact and supported the status quo.

What was the status quo? – Well, put quite simply; boys got jobs in engineering, if they were clever then they might be lucky enough to go to university, if not, they would get an apprenticeship. Girls would go on to do a basic secretarial course, work for three or four years, then get married (to an engineer!) and have a succession of children fairly quickly. This was the 1960s, swinging London and its exotic fashions was very far away, so far away it might as well have been swinging Jamaica for all that we could possibly hope to even visit it.

The library though, was a refuge. I could go and stay out of my parents' hair, whilst apparently reading sensible books. They would have been horrified and I would have been severely punished, if they had realised that I spent the hours between school and tea-time, tucked behind the far corner of the adult section, reading psychology and medical texts. It was in those dark corners that I discovered sexuality, gender and their difference.

I was very fortunate to win a scholarship, much to my father's annoyance, to a girls' public school. It proved to be a mixed blessing. It was situated a few minutes from home. As such, it took the brunt of the local kids' jokes and as a local kid, it was in many ways, to isolate me further from my home community. However, I can with pride say that the school philosophy – which was to make successful women of us, made me the man I am today. I often wonder if the school staff and my fellow pupils ever realised what a source of sanity they were to me. Nobody expected me to be anybody but myself and that must have been a strange mix for them to try and understand.

I was popular, but didn't have close friends. I was hard working and enthusiastic, but never very successful. I became cricket captain, house captain and deputy head girl, yet I know I didn't fit in. The school was a place of tolerance, it was proud to have an ethos of no punishment and no praise, yet its Marxist (I am sure they would not have ever conceded that they were) principles of equal opportunities never deterred it from the task of making sure that we could leave it as successful and confident achievers.

It was a period in my life of contradictions, I also wanted to achieve at what the school offered, yet I didn't want to achieve it their way. I knew, in the same way that one knows God and has faith, that I had to become a man, not a woman, in order to become anybody.

I was seventeen years old when my journey to Damascus was to take place. It took place in the local doctor's surgery and the blinding flash of light was in the form of a woman's magazine. I can remember to this day, the image presented before me of a donkey-jacketed figure passing through a garden gate. It was the story of a woman who had a sex change and became a man. I knew now that it was possible, I could find a way of living. I also knew that it was not something I could discuss with anyone. This was 1971, flares and hot pants may have made it to the grimy north west, but sexual liberation certainly hadn't.

For about six weeks I became physically ill, I lost all my balance mechanisms. I couldn't face having to live another day as "nobody". Physical aspects of my "femaleness" were abhorrent, and coping with them for any longer seemed impossible. It took me the six weeks of lying flat on my back to work out where to go next. I decided that I was an intelligent being, I knew there were several routes open to me: living as a woman or living as a man, becoming androgynous, or, if nothing else worked out, I could always choose death. I had tried already to kill myself a couple of times and done nothing more than make myself very sick, so now seemed the time to try the other options.

I chose what seemed the easiest first – to live as a woman. This, I reckoned could be possible if I sorted out ways to live the life of a liberated woman and to that end, I chose to go to teacher training college, away from home. It was here that I slept around. I tried male and female partners, I tried to be whom they wanted. However, sleeping with women proved to be very difficult because they wanted to like the body I hated. Sleeping with men was better – they didn't care whether they liked your body or not, their main aim was to get their end away and the less they had to touch you to get that, the better. But it was fraught with fear – of pregnancy, of maybe having to get married, of becoming known as an easy lay. I wasn't sure of what to do, until my first teaching practice and it came to light (and remember this was the early seventies) that I would have to wear a skirt or dress to work every day. That did it, and I left.

I was to spend the next couple of years drifting from job to job, I suppose, in an androgynous state. At one stage I was homeless and slept in the park for the summer. But I knew what I was looking for: I had decided that I had to become a man.

I found it, ironically through the Women's Movement and a radical lesbian feminist group, to whom I finally confessed my desperate need to live as a man. I was astonished by their reaction – instead of spurning me, they searched through their wardrobes for their jackets and ties. They dressed me as a man, they drew a moustache on my upper lip and they took me to the most alternative club they could find in the city, where they introduced me to a very good looking woman called Carol, who turned out to be a man undergoing sex reassignment.

Here was living proof, through Carol and the Manchester TV/TS group, I met another guy like myself. Nick lived with his "wife" and "their" baby and he maybe wasn't all that respectable, being something of a wide boy, but he became a friend, a friend who took me in and introduced me to his friends as if I was already a man.

I got my GP, Greta to refer me to a local specialist in gender identity disorders. He turned out to be a megalomaniac psychiatrist who, after numerous

Lovers – Photograph by Jim Stagg

The American Lawyer,
Phyllis Randolph Frye

The End of Silence

Dr. Stephen Whittle – Senior Lecturer in Law at Manchester University

Vicky – Girls will be Girls

Madame Alexia

A Moment of Contemplation

Beverley marches for her rights

A Hijra

Judd and his wife – Photograph by Del Grace

The fabulous Natasha shows off her rollerskates

Marjorie is a Native American Blackfoot Sioux

Alexander – Photograph by Del Grace

DJ, Mother Pearl E. Monsoon explains the trannie facts of life to actress Margie Clarke

Tracie and Katrina – two's trouble

Cowboy Jordan – Photograph by Del Grace

Fay Presto, the magician. Lesbian, Gay, Bisexual & Transgender Pride March 1996

Alex of Press for Change

The lovely Kim

investigations, told me that I would never hack it as a man. He's still in my little black book and made me the nearest to suicide I've ever been since. Greta though, had the foresight to realise how close I was to the edge and came round to my very grotty flat and wrote out a prescription for hormones. Things have never looked back since – well, in reality they have. I was made very uncomfortable at work, but the gay shop steward enabled me to keep my job whilst I transitioned. I've been sacked from another job because I had had a sex change. It took four years of binding my chest before I got surgery. My father can still barely look me in the face and yet. . . .

I have now been living as a guy for almost twenty years. I am a successful university lecturer, I have the most wonderful and understanding woman at my side who has weathered the storms with me for almost sixteen of those years, we have two beautiful children, conceived by artificial insemination and more than ever, I am determined to fight for my right to be myself.

I am now a very public figure in the transsexual world. I have learnt that blood isn't thicker than water and that loved ones do not have to be related. I now like and fancy people because of what's between their ears, not what's between their legs and I have a few regrets. But those regrets are so few – I look at my children and am thankful that they will hopefully never feel the despair that I did, of an unwanted gender. Yet I cannot help but wonder whether my son will be half the man because he cannot possibly hope to learn the things that I have learnt. I have become a whole person, I have made the ultimate choice to be exactly who I am. As such, I can now make any other choice and I know that, given the determination and the hard work, all things are possible.

Alex (mascusexual)

As a child I wouldn't have had the right words to express the confusion of growing up transsexual. But every time I had the right to wish (on stars, wells, Christmas puddings, wishbones. . .) I automatically wished to be a boy. I think this desire was clear by the time I was about three.

I wasn't especially unhappy as a child. My parents tolerated my tomboy inclinations, and let me wear boys clothes out of school. My friends called me "Kay", which was short for my real name, but gender ambiguous. I felt I had to prove myself, for my own self respect as well as for the respect of others. By a combination of extreme recklessness and some skill in fighting, I won the status of a kind of honorary boy. My role models were George from the Famous Five and the boy-girl in West Side Story. When I was ten, I persuaded my mother to let me have a crew cut. Strangers assumed me to be a boy, which pleased me greatly. But despite all the wishes and the vivid dreams in which the wishes came true, my penis never grew. Instead, as I passed the age at which normal girls grow out of grey socks and war games, pressure mounted from all quarters for me to conform.

Puberty was final and horrifying confirmation that I really wasn't going to become a boy. From a sociable and cheerful (if rather a strange) child, I became violently unhappy and withdrawn. I was excluded from school because of my disruptive behaviour. I suffered strange symptoms – hysterical paralysis and colour blindness. My parents worried and they did their best. They took me to the GP, who prescribed female hormones (which I washed down the sink) and then to a child psychiatrist, who provisionally diagnosed schizophrenia. Eventually I was referred to a residential psychiatric unit, where I became scared enough of what might happen to me to pull myself together. I went home and did my best to act normally, resigned to the idea that I was different from other people.

I would like to believe that one day transsexual children could be diagnosed and supported, if not actually treated, before they reach puberty. I think my story is fairly typical – I have heard other transsexuals tell of their utter despair during this period of their lives.

When I was nineteen years old, I spent part of my long

summer holiday from university walking on the north Cornish coast. While walking I did some hard thinking. It had become obvious to me that I could not live the rest of my life as a woman. Two serious alternatives suggested themselves: suicide or life as a man. I resolved to attempt to live as a man, with suicide as a fallback position, should this prove impossible.

I was probably rather more ignorant of human sexuality and gender than many of my contemporaries, having deliberately renounced participation in the courtship rituals of adolescence, during which most people seem to become sexually streetwise. Instead I had spent the last five or six years developing a rather impressive ability to play the piano. However, I had seen a television documentary in which ewes injected with testosterone developed some of the physical characteristics of rams and wondered whether the same could be done for people. I had also heard of gay and lesbian people and considered that I must be something along those lines. On my return to university I rang the Gay Switchboard, whose number was to be found on the toilet wall and explained my problem. This was the first time I heard the word "transsexual" and I knew at once that this was what I was.

My relief in discovering that I was not alone in the world was slightly tempered when I attended the TV/TS group at the university chaplaincy with a view to obtaining further information. I had led a sheltered life and was absolutely stunned to walk into a room full of big men in make-up and frilly frocks. They turned out to be transvestites, something I had never heard of and were terribly motherly. They insisted I should wait, as Steve would be along later. Steve turned out be a skinny lad with an Alsation pup on a string. He was also a female-to-male transsexual. He showed me how to bind my breasts, advised me to get a hair-cut and explained how to legally change my name. Within the week I had had my sex change. I felt better immediately.

I had no problems passing as a fourteen year old boy and enjoyed a year of unsolicited half fares on public transport, only too glad to be called "son" by conductors. After six months I persuaded a sympathetic GP to prescribe hormones – available for people as well as sheep. As the hormones took effect, my voice slid from soprano to bass, forcing me to learn all four vocal parts of the Mozart Requiem in quick succession in order to remain in the choir. I began to shave, the humiliating periods stopped for good and my body regained its childhood hardness and energy. After jumping through some psychiatric hoops (during which, no hint was found of my supposed "schizophrenia"), I was referred for a mastectomy to an excellent surgeon and had the operation four years after changing over – quite quickly for those days. Phalloplasty was not on offer. I then got on with my life.

Nobody who knew me seemed surprised to hear I had had a sex change. My father wondered if I should have taken more time to think about it and my mother cried, because she thought I would be an outcast. But as it became obvious that I was happy with myself for the first time in years and leading a full and successful life by anyone's standards, they accepted it. My mother in particular was very proud of me and claimed she had always wanted a son. I suspect this was a fib, but it was nice of her to say so. I didn't exactly lose friends from having a sex change. It is more that they had already been lost or not made in the first place, as a result of my teenage years of alienation. But I have made plenty of friends since. Close friends and colleagues know I am transsexual and I do not make a secret of it if the subject arises. On the other hand, being transsexual isn't central to my everyday life.

The changeover took place nineteen years ago – I have now lived half my life as a man. I have a good job which I enjoy, working for a Housing Association and a comfortable middle class lifestyle. I don't have a partner – my decision that this is not for me still stands – but I live with a group of friends. I am a responsible and respected member of society. I suppose I am a good advertisement for gender reassignment as a quick and permanently effective cure for the misery of being transsexual.

I have no regrets over my sex change, as without this solution I imagine I would have been dead or mad. However, it would be dishonest to pretend that everything is fine. Although my experience has given me valuable insights and perhaps even made me a better person, I wouldn't go so far as to say I'm glad or proud to be transsexual, or that the unhappiness it caused me was somehow worthwhile. If I could choose again, I would want to be born a physically normal boy.

But all in all I consider myself very lucky. Being transsexual is a misfortune, but it is no worse than many other problems that people live with. The secret is to enjoy and value what you have and live life as fully as possible. I try not to waste time in regrets over what might have been in some "other life" – after all, we only live once and nobody ever said it had to be fair!

Dan (mascusexual)

"All I could see standing next to me was a man, so smart in your shirt and tie, and to top it all, I was so proud of you".

This was my mother's most distressing realisation that the child she gave birth to all those years ago is in fact a young man. So, here I am now, Daniel, a thirty five year old civil engineer complete with a young son. It is now ten months since I opened the can of worms that I had been suppressing unsuccessfully since puberty. Four months ago I stepped into the world of men as a man.

This period of time has been filled to the brim with a combination of happiness, contentment, hilarity, trauma and despair from others, but above all, total love leading to understanding from those closest to me. My "coming out" was not easy, I doubt it ever is – so much worry and anxiety that I would be rejected by everyone around me. However my fears were not realised with most of my friends, following a period of constant interrogation, accepting me. For many my acknowledgement of gender dysphoria has explained so much of my previous behaviour.

Now the hardest part for me is meeting people that I

knew before both socially and professionally. I have driven to site, worried about the attitude of labourers there and have arrived to find all and sundry calling me Dan. I then worry about what they have been told, and who told them! I am also having to reappraise my own past. How can I admit attending an all girls' school? How can I admit to having male partners? How can I justify the time off work having my son? It's a real journey travelling forward, not just psychologically and physically, but to rework where I have come from. I do not wish to deny my past, however, to be totally accepted as Daniel I must be able to answer all the questions that new acquaintances ask with ease.

I have become involved with some unusual research – my voice is being monitored during its break for comparison against genetic boys. My employers are unwittingly involved in forming my male body by default in engaging health and fitness experts to help employees with diet and exercise.

As for my son, it is a lot for a nine year old to take in: he is a great ally. If he had the opportunity, I think I would own every tie with an animal pattern and plenty of shirts to grow into. He insists on leading the way into the Gents so he can check where the cubicles are.

In retrospect, if I had known that I could face up to my confusion and the future with so much support, I would have come out earlier. But there is a time and place for everything and my time is now.

Shadow (mascusexual)

I am constantly reminded, in everything I do in life, about my "situation". I am a man who was born with the genital structure of a female. The doctors call me a transsexual. I refer to myself as a metamorph. My life today is a focus on who I am. What kind of man am I? Do I have to buy into the stereotypes of men? Have I bought into some of those stereotypes already? What can I do to be the best human being that I can possibly be? What is my responsibility to others as I journey?

There are so many things that make up who I am. Yes, my being a metamorph is a large part of how I function in the world, but it is not the whole of me. If anyone chooses to focus solely on that one aspect of my life, then they are cheating both of us. How can they possibly know who I am based off of one piece of me? I try to meet each new person in my life as an individual; a new experience that could lead to an adventure of new discoveries, new conflicts, new friendship, or a chance to simply connect with another human being. My biggest hope is that others will try to meet me with a similar openness.

The part of my path that deals with my being a metamorph has by no means been an easy journey. But it continuously feeds me new adventures every day of my life. The sum and total of all those experiences, joyful and difficult, exciting and dangerous, has made me the person that I am in this moment. I like who I am.

Danielle (femisexual)
When you are a child you don't think in clinical terms and it is difficult to define when I knew I was female. The best I can say is that since I can remember, I had a strong need to express my female self. At about the age of eleven, I became aware that I was different. To have a need to express myself naturally and to have that thwarted and be made to feel guilty about it made me implode. I was in my own little world, oblivious to much of what went on around me. It took time to find out what and who I was. When I found out it took time to accept, but once I sought help, things began to fall into place.

I was lost until I met another transsexual who I have had a relationship with for over three years. I followed her lead and went to a psychiatrist in Earl's Court. After consulting him, I went on to a course of hormone therapy and also started electrolysis. After about three years I was referred to a surgeon and my operation took place on 3rd March 1994 in Brighton. I have been very happy with my treatment. I am pleased with my general appearance and am particularly over the moon about my newly constructed vagina, both in its appearance and function. I chose a private route for my change, including the reassignment surgery. I support the idea of the NHS completely and would have liked to have been able to use them. I would have done this if transsexuals were seen by those in charge as real patients with a recognised and potentially fatal condition, if untreated.

When I was a child I was very close to my mother. She would hug me and tell how much she loved me. The trouble started as my feminine self became stronger. At eighteen years old I regularly wore make-up and this caused a lot of friction. Only my youngest sister seemed not to judge me. My frustration and confusion about my gender, body and sexuality nearly drove me over the edge. In the end I feared for my mother's safety as I became increasingly aggressive.

I began to cross dress regularly and tried to hide it from my youngest sister. This is strange because I never hid anything from her until this point, but something about cross-dressing made me too scared, ashamed even to tell her. This drove a wedge between us and I began to lose her. Only when I went away and started the change was I able to come back and tell her about it. My sister has two young children who were babies when I started the change and they have been the most unconditional in their acceptance of me as Danielle.

I have no regrets as far as I did the right thing for my health. I do regret losing the love of my mother and causing her so much pain before I sorted my head and body out. The future is, as always, uncertain. Transsexuals have no rights in the UK. If I found a job, I could be sacked for being transsexual and would have no legal redress. Reactions to me vary. When someone knows I am transsexual they are surprised because when they think of a transsexual, they usually think of them being like a transvestite or drag queen with layers of make-up, wearing a micro skirt, high heels and a bad wig.

In ordinary every-day life I live and am accepted as female and function quite well. My background is working class, although as transsexuals are less than third class in terms of human rights, I personally don't think I have a class any more. I am currently unemployed.

There are many answers to transsexualism. My answer was to take hormones, have electrolysis and finally gender reassignment. Others suppress how they feel or seek a cure for their transsexualism through other forms of counselling and/or drug therapy, some live and work as women or men, but don't go all the way. There is no answer for everyone, only what the individual feels is right for them.

Catheryn (femisexual)

I was born in New Zealand in 1949. It is an odd feeling reflecting back over my life. I am one week away from my forty seventh birthday and it has taken this long to come to terms with the rationality of my young thoughts. Society tends to victimise that which cannot be understood, at any level. My earliest recollection of being "different" was at the age of five when some local boys threw stones at me. The physical, and in some ways, the emotional, scar still exists. They gave no verbal abuse, offered no reason for the attack; it just happened. However, it did clarify something for me. I "was" different. How different did not materialise until the age of six when sitting in my classroom I envied the girls with their dolls, clothing, their play. I just so wanted to join in with them. Isolation was a reality for me and it is that scar which, perhaps, sits just as strong with me today as it did then.

Somebody was making a very bad mistake. Why did "they" not give me a tablet. The tablet was my way of accepting the moment. I firmly believed that girls were given a tablet to make them girls. "They", whoever they may be, simply hadn't given me mine. No matter, one day "they" will realise their mistake. Once the "tablet" phase had passed, around the age of thirteen, I then would dream about the surgery which would give me the femaleness I

141

craved. I wanted to have boyfriends, share girl talk, isolation still very much a major part of my life. At this stage I was involved with ballet, starting at the age of seven. This only aided to my being "different", but I would not give it up. In the ballet world, I felt "normal".

After the school years, I quickly assimilated with the gay community. This felt home to me, on one level only. I still was not being viewed as female. I first moved to Wellington when I was nineteen with some gay friends. The year was 1969 and my friends decided to show me what a drag queen looked like. I had no idea what they were talking about. At the end of the night they asked me what I had thought of the drag queens. I hadn't any thoughts. I did notice a group of glamorous women, however. When it was explained to me they were drag queens, men in frocks, my mind did a 360 degree turn. I was home. The next night I threw together what clothes could pass as female, short hair and very simple makeup. I was both delighted and horrified that I had not been recognised as a drag queen. The next night it was explained to me, everyone thought I was female.

I left Wellington and returned again in 1972 quickly securing a job as a dancer and hostess for Carmen's Balcony and Coffee Bar. I also worked as a street prostitute (sex worker) until I left Wellington in 1977. In 1978 I had the sex change operation and moved to Brisbane, Australia. There I worked as a sex worker in a massage parlour and eventually a private escort. At the same time I was learning ice skating to keep my body in good condition. I had learned as a child and now as an adult I resat my exams.

A client of mine decided I should leave the industry and talked me into moving in with him. Soon after I was hired as a skating coach where I also performed in local ice shows. The ice rink I worked at closed so my partner and I moved to Bredbo, 70kms outside of Canberra, where we started an Angora Goat Stud. I also worked as a skating coach in Canberra and performed in a local ice show, which was a major annual event. In 1989 my partner died soon after I had started studying for my Bachelors Degree at the University of Canberra. I graduated in 1992 with a Bachelor of Applied Science, in Health Education, majoring in Biological Science and Health Education. I sub majored in Sociology. After graduating I sold the farm and returned to New Zealand where I work for the New Zealand Prostitutes' Collective as a Health Educator.

Much of my life has been hiding my gender from others. My aim is to work more with transgender groups and work as a support for those moving through these processes. So the rationality of my young thoughts? Expecting "them" to realise their mistake. It has taken until now to understand "they" never made a mistake. It is up to me to understand my normalness, not for anyone else. "They" are already basking in "theirs", whatever that may be. For that I say: "I am me, I am here, and I am OK".

Vicky (femisexual)

I was born a healthy boy, in 1959 in my parents' bed. My early years were very happy. Myself and my sister, who is five years older than me were much loved. I can remember at the age of six or seven, I started to become envious of my sister, because of all the lovely dolls she had and also the pretty dresses she wore. Very often this would lead me to fight with her, she would end up crying and I would get a smack from my dad for wanting to play with girls' toys.

At school I was always to be found with the girls, playing skipping or other feminine games. The boys were always too rough for me and I hated football. Anyway, I got through Junior school, but the nightmare was just beginning. I was off to secondary school. Every day I was kicked, spat at and verbally abused, just because I acted like a girl, but I can assure you, acting never came into it. My femininity was quite natural and I can remember going into sweet-shops and the owner saying "Can I help you, little girl?" I would leave the shop with my sherbet lemons, feeling totally confused. My dad, you see, would drum it into me that I was a boy and boys did this and girls did

143

that. Perhaps boys didn't have sherbet lemons, I was left thinking.

Anyway, I plodded away at school through my teens, wanting to wear glitter under my eyes, like Marc Bolan of T-Rex, who was my idol at that time. Another thing that confused me at this time was the way the boys at school called me names when they were in groups. However, when they were on their own with me, in a quiet corridor or stairwell at school, they wanted me to touch them down below, which I was only too pleased to do, if it saved me a kicking.

I left school when I was sixteen and I got a job on British Rail, serving tea and coffee on the 8.15am London to Glasgow Express. I did this work for three years and enjoyed it. During this time, however, I had left home and moved into a flat of my own. Also, I had been going to a gay pub on a regular basis, where I saw many drag shows. I would stand and watch these men in sequinned frocks and high heels, knowing I could do it and better, so that's what I did. I became the glamorous "Vicky Vamp". I looked just like one of my sister's dolls and I loved it.

One night, in the pub after I had finished my show I got talking to a stunning lady, who had been in the audience. After a while she told me that she was once a drag artist like me. I couldn't believe it, she was lovely. She went on to explain to me how she had gone about becoming the woman she always knew she was. Afterwards I knew just what I wanted to do. I was determined change from a caterpillar in sequins to a butterfly in silk.

My GP was very good and gave me a letter for Charing Cross Hospital and also a prescription for female hormones. Never again would I dress as a boy. After seeing a psychiatrist every three months for three years, I was eventually put on a waiting list for surgery. It was at this time that I met the love of my life, Steve. We met at a club and he made me feel so at ease, so I explained everything about myself to him. After the initial shock he smiled his sexy smile and told me he liked me for me and was willing to wait until I was ready for a physical relationship. Two years passed and one bright, sunny morning a letter from the hospital arrived. I had a date for my operation. It was the best moment of my life and I danced around the flat like a little girl. I will never forget that day.

My operation was a complete success and the love of my life, Steve is still with me ten years on. I have also now had breast implants and no longer take hormones, which can make you feel quite moody. I thank my whole family for accepting me and helping me get through my troubled times. My mother is very special to me. People tell me that I look like her and that's the greatest compliment I could have, because she is beautiful and I thank her for making my life that much easier.

Cynthia (not everyone wants surgery!)

It would appear that from an early age all of us of the Transgendered know we are different but cannot come to grips with just how different until our later years. I am no different than any other Transgendered person, come to think of it I am no different than any other human being on this beautiful planet. What I am is unique as all people are but, I am different even unto the Transgendered community. My name is Cynthia Roberts and this is my condensed story.

I was born into a military family in the late '50s and from the time I was born we were always moving around to new and exotic far away places. Being exposed to all the different cultures, religions and lifestyles gave me a look at the world different than most growing children. I came to the realisation early on that there is no absolute right, nor is there ever an absolute wrong for anything, only shades of interpretation. It was as a teenager in Taiwan, that I first came to understand that I was more of a girl than a boy. It started with borrowing mom's clothes and dressing up. This lasted through three countries and five different schools. I still did not know who or what I was but, I was learning, from experience and reading.

My real test and first purge was when I turned 18 and lived as a woman for three weeks in Florida. At the end of the three weeks, I purged so hard I joined the military. Not just any military but, I had to go hard core and join the US Army and go through Parachute training and then Ranger school to become a real rough tough fighting machine. I was considered good enough to be selected to attend advanced weapons training and Sniper school. This really buried my inner female. My enlistment lasted four years. Upon discharge I turned to the burgeoning oilfield to make a living, again a hard road to go but, a necessary one. You see I was still in denial that I was somehow different. Throughout this time I had not touched anything remotely feminine unless it was attached to a Gender female and that for only a short interlude.

Five years ago after going through many long years of suppressing my inner self, I subjected myself to counselling and then medical tests to find out about these powerful urges and feelings that I should have been a girl instead of a boy. In other words what was "wrong" with me. The diagnosis was interesting, I was told that I was a Transsexual, that I should have been born a girl! What a blow to the ego! It took an additional year to come to the understanding that I knew all along I was female but did not want to face the reality of the situation. It has been three and a half years now in transition and I am well balanced and happy. I still have a stereotypical male job but I perform it as what I am, not quite a woman in the biological sense but close enough. Sexual Reassignment Surgery is not in the picture. I have developed an understanding within myself that the androgyny of having both minds occupying one body and interacting in society as female is too much fun to exchange for a one sided lifestyle. So I will remain within both worlds never completely part of either but unique unto myself. I guess this was where my life was going all along, I am a product of my environment and my biology. Not too bad actually if you can handle the psychological turmoil it sometimes results in.

Samantha (pre-femisexual)

I was the oldest of three boys and always the one expected to succeed just like my father who owned a trucking company. Driving a truck was something that came natural and I never really thought of it as a girl or boy thing. No one at school would have dared to call me a sissy and lived to tell the tale.

As far back as I can remember Rosie was my sweetheart and we'd fish, ride horses and race track bikes together. She was tough and my best friend, so when at eighteen I married her in the town church, no one suspected my innermost feelings I had about being a girl. Back in those days I didn't know you could fix such things and I never told anyone in case they thought me crazy.

I'm glad I had two kids with Rosie and I'll never regret it, but the sex stuff was sure more than I could handle. I guess friendship was our best ally, but there are some things I just couldn't share with her. It was easy away from home to be Samantha since sometimes Rosie wouldn't expect me for days. I felt sort of guilty not being able to tell her the truth but I couldn't help myself – I just had to be me.

You don't tell these sort of things to a doctor in a small town you've lived in all your life, but the folks at the gender clinic I started to attend understood. After five years since we were married, I'd learnt so much about who I was inside and who I needed to be but I just didn't want to hurt Rosie and the kids. The only way out was to tell her and leave. After the initial shock because she didn't even know what a transsexual was, she took it personal and went ballistic. I can't blame her for being angry because I'm angry too that this happened to me.

It's been five years now since I left them and I'm going into surgery next month. Of course I still own the trucks and send money home even though Rosie's got a new guy. It seems sort of right as no matter what, I'm still a parent, even though I don't see my kids. I'm happy as Samantha even though there's nobody special in my life. It's a bit like being a teenager again and finding my way in the world.

147

Some day I hope they'll understand and then perhaps we can all be friends again. The doctor tell me it's no one's fault and I'm getting used to that now, but it sure has been a messy time.

Nowadays a woman trucker isn't such a big thing and what with the hormones I don't look like I used to. I'm sort of hoping life begins again at twenty eight and I know I've still got a lot of work to do on myself. I'm getting there, bit by bit, piece by piece. Nothing's going to stop me, nothing can be done about the past and if I haven't got myself, I haven't got any future. So, I'm going to be me first and hopefully folks'll love me for that – Samantha, Queen of the Road.

Sandy (Some people change their mind)

I remember being sixteen, at college with other girls and not having a sense of belonging. My two brothers were rough and tumble and I'd grown up like that too. My mum and dad had grown up on a farm in Yugoslavia and found nothing odd about a daughter who chopped logs, played with her brothers and worked on the farm.

I'd been pushed into hairdressing at college because my parents thought it was the girly sort of thing that I needed to develop me into a young lady. I, on the other hand, was happy as Larry in jeans, boots and leather jacket, messing around with my motor bike. Everyone had called me Sandy, because of the colour of my hair and the strange thing is, the androgyny of the name naturally extended itself to my tomboy personality. Wherever my brothers went, I wasn't very far behind.

I hated being called "she" and I was convinced that I was a boy. Haircurling and lipstick was definitely not for me. I don't say I didn't have fun putting it on other girls, but for me, no thank you very much. Mum and dad began to get worried when I was about sixteen, but now they say before that they'd taken my tomboy ways as being quite natural. I was dispatched off to a psychiatrist who promptly told me I'd grow out of it and if not, to change my major from hairdressing to mechanics. This was the most thrilling advice I think I'd ever had in my life up till then.

Up to the elbows in axle grease I spent the next three years under cars, lorries, motorbikes and anything with wheels that promised to go bang, fast and ferocious. All the other mechanics just treated me like one of the boys and that was OK for me, because that's what I felt I was. Although now I had the kind of lifestyle I wanted, I felt no need to become myself, more male than I was.

As I approached twenty, a new mechanic came to work at the same garage as me and he was the kind of mate whom I felt I could have fun with. A special bond grew between us which developed into a sound and solid friendship. We went away on holiday together, several times and to race meetings, where sometimes I'd enter one of my motorbikes and other times he'd enter one of his. It was hardly what I could describe as a blossoming romance, but one thing led to the next and before I knew where I was, the loss of my virginity had turned into pregnancy.

Bobby, as he was called, has never let me down and people find us an odd couple, never knowing which one of us is driving up the road in our crash helmets, but I'm happy and I'm me and I'm no different from what I ever felt I was. Although now I'm a mum with two children, I still work in the garage part-time and I still feel male, compared to other women. I've never worn a dress, lipstick or put my hair in curls and I don't particularly fancy men, but Bobby's different somehow. It's not so much sex as friendship.

The psychiatrist asked me if I fancied girls. Well! I like them a lot, but I don't know if I'd ever want to sleep with one and the funny thing is, that's the way I feel about men too. I don't think I want to be a man now, it seems to have worn off, but I don't really think of myself as a woman either, just me, whatever I am?"

Marjorie Anne Napewa̒stewiñ Schützer (Paper reproduced given to the ENPT Conference 1994)

I am "Sihasapa", "Lakota" or rather that is to say that I am of the Blackfoot tribe. We are one of seven tribes of the Sioux nation. I am Native American. An old Lakota word, "Winyanktehca" has today been contracted to the simple word, "Winkte" meaning, "two-souls-person" or more directly meaning "to be as a woman". (I would like to suggest that in this speech, I will make use of the word "Winkte" synonymously for "gender crosser" in either direction.) I am "Wakan" – to my people I am sacred and mysterious, I am a spirit person. The Grandfathers tell me this. I have my feet rooted in the earth of my ancestors and my spirit soars with them in the "land above the pines". The anthropologists call me "Berdache" but this is wrong. This word has come a long way from its beginnings in Arabia. It means "kept boy". . . that I am not. The Western medical community calls me "transsexual", but this is not entirely true either. I am "Winkte", I am a gender-crosser. My people see me as multidimensional and I do not have to fight for a place in my society to be accepted. I already have a place, a very special and sacred place. In my culture I represent a profound healing, a reconciliation of the most fundamental rift that divides us, human from human – gender.

I was called through a vision, by "Anog Ite", (Double Face Woman) from out of the womb, to that which I am. She offered me a choice. Lakota deities never order. My gender transformation was called for by the Spirits. She blessed me with skills of a supernatural kind. One of our "Wicasa Wakan" or Medicine Men of today, John Lame Deer, says in his book, "Lame Deer, Seeker of Visions", "Wintke are men who dress like women, look like women and act like women. They do so by their own choice or in obedience to a dream. They are not like other men, but "Wakan Tanka", the Great Spirit, made them "Wintkes" and we accept them as such. To us a man is what nature, or his dreams, make him. We accept him for what he wants to be. That's up to him. In our tribe we go to a "Wintke" to give a new born child a secret name. They have the gift of prophecy, and the secret name a "Wintkte" gives to a child is believed to be especially powerful and effective. In former days a father gave a "Wintke" a fine horse in return for such a name. If nature puts a burden on a person, it also gives a power and that which I produce with my hands is "highly desirable". Anog Ite has set my feet on both sides of the "line" and I can see into the hearts of both men and women. We are hunters and we keep the house, we cook and do beadwork. I . . . have chosen the path I have walked. In the Lakota language there are no personal pronouns and a child is simply a child until the age of four or five, when he or she shows that which they are. I have a place also, in this . . . your society.

My people have always held their "Wintke" in awe and reverence and before the "white man" came to the "new world" we were many. But our numbers shrank and we began to hide within ourselves as our religious systems were attacked and shattered by western attitudes. Because of the impact of white ridicule we had all but disappeared. Because of the enormous difference between European societies and Native American societies, differences which theoretically rules out any comparison of their respective sex and gender roles, we must ask ourselves, "What is being lost?" Is it possible that within a Native American interpretation we see something that a Western point of view cannot? Being Lakota, I know myself as something precious and the dignity in such knowing pulls me to my full tallness. Being "Wintke" however, allows me the full capability of achieving a strong ego identity, originality, and an active inner life, which is characteristic of adult individuation and personality development.

We are "shamans". We are called upon to bestow secret and powerful names on the new born, names which represent "long-life" and which could lead to fame. Sitting Bull, Black Elk, even Crazy Horse had a secret name which only a few people knew. These names are often very sexy, even funny, very outspoken. You don't let a stranger know them; he would kid you about it! We were consulted to divine the success of proposed battles. We were tied closely to the war complex, we were even a crucial part of it. We treated the wounded; we had custody of the scalps and carried these into camp. We ran the victory dance that followed the raiders' return. Some tribal councils decided nothing without our advice. We were called upon to conduct burials. There are certain cures and uses for herbs known only to "Wintkes". The most sacred of our ceremonies, the Sun Dance, could not begin without our selecting and raising the poles to be used. But even more significant it was believed that our power could extend beyond the individual to affect others. The prosperity and even their existence as a people, in some Native American Societies depended upon their "Wintke". One of the major aspects which distinguishes "Wintke" in our native culture, is a preference for the work of the other sex. This key trait, in the Native American perspective was perhaps of the least importance to western society, since whites do not value women's worth anyway. The crossing of these boundaries requires an unusually strong endowment with power . . . and those who allow themselves to see us with their spirit eyes . . . they can see this.

What has Western civilization lost by its apparent lack of a counterpart to "Wintke" by, indeed, bending every social institution to the task of stigmatising gender mediation? More than the waste of the individual's potential which suppression entails, there is the loss of the "Wintke spirit guide" who serves men and women alike with the insights of the intermediate position. This raises the question whether men and women today can ever achieve mutuality and wholeness, as long as men who manifest qualities considered feminine, and women who do the same in male realms, are seen as deviants to be criminalised and stigmatised. The fear of being associated with this deviant status stands before every man and woman who would seek psychic integration, regardless of their emotional and sexual orientation. It is made all too apparent through the observation that in societies which make a minimum use of sex as a discriminating factor in prescribing behaviour, as opposed to those that maximise sex distinction, that we see "Wintkes" become not only open and prevalent, but even necessary. Western images of men and women are not as flexible as "oyte ikce" (native people). Violent outbursts of hatred or anger towards "Wintke" comparable to expressions of western homophobia have never been recorded in Native American history. However, a biological and not a social definition of gender continues to inform both popular and scientific western thinking. But being male biologically and "acting like a man" are not necessarily the same thing.

"Wintke" are not branded as threats to a rigid gender ideology; but rather we are considered an affirmation of humanity's original pre-gendered unity – we are representatives of a form of solidarity and wholeness which transcends the division of humans into men and women. "Wintke" transformation was not, and is not, a complete shift from his or her biological gender to the opposite one, but rather an approximation of the latter in some of its social, and of course today, its physical aspects, effecting an intermediate status that cuts across the boundaries between gender categories. As long as our perceptions continue to be filtered through a dual gender ideology and arbitrary distinctions based on biological sex are held, "Wintke" patterns cannot be appreciated of what they really are. That is, the appropriate and intrinsic behaviour of one or the other of the two "real" genders, an imitation which is invariably found inferior and counterfeit. Those behaviours inappropriate for an individual's biological sex, like cross-dressing, are consequently singled out. But comparisons of male to female "Wintke" to women, invariably reveal more about the speaker's view of women (usually a negative one) than they do about "Wintke". In light of the "discovery" of the third gender, all such accounts must be re-evaluated. Everyone can take inspiration from a society where individuality and community are not always at odds.

In our work we must remember . . . the most important

objective we are called upon to realise with our clients is to make available to them this sense of wholeness and inner solidarity. In fact that very wholeness and solidarity which all humans are seeking. It is only through our understanding that "Wintke" status transcends the boundaries of a gender category that is biologically and not culturally and socially defined, that we attain an intermediate gender status, biologically the same but culturally redefined. In many ways, socially, legally, psychologically and even in this day and age, physiologically, western tradition still ignores the individual motivations of our "Wintke", stressing instead categories and labels for these people in the name of our own convenience.

Such sexual diversity has always been considered one sign of a lower social development. In fact, the response of 19th century Victorian America. Like the Spaniards before them, to native sexuality is much the same as we see world wide today and this exposes in everyone of us, a central contradiction in our basic belief system. In fact when seen in the light of traditional Native American values it is impossible to rely entirely on a western analysis without distorting this fantastic phenomenon altogether. This is, without a doubt they key where "Wintke" itself must be understood if one is to comprehend the reasons individuals adopt it.

With the recognition of the third gender status the problem of the transsexual or the gender-crosser model becomes clear. For example, the man who becomes a woman contributes to society as a woman. But with a deep understanding of the "Wintke" position, new unique and rare contributions to society become possible. Society can only benefit by recognising three, instead of two, genders. Such a reorganisation of gender geometrically increases options for individual identities and behaviours. The third gender role of "Wintke", one which has existed openly within the framework of everyday Lakota culture, is one of native North America's most striking social inventions.

At one time, I believed it was a wise person who was able to recognise their own limitations and was then able to operate within those limitations. However I am now convinced that quite the contrary shall be considered as the fact. It is rather the wise person who is able to be aware of all of their own possibilities and to then operate at the outer limits of those possibilities. We owe it to our profession, to our clients and to ourselves, to recognise our own possibilities and then in response to that recognition to move ourselves around the "medicine wheel" of life so as to experience those who come to us for help while we ourselves are standing at a different vantage point, my challenge to you today . . . is to simply . . . "think primitive".

PARTNERS, FRIENDS AND RELATIVES
Katrina Fox (Tracie's partner)

I met Tracie just over three years ago at a small social gathering. At the time, I was a self-proclaimed lesbian, although I had not been in any kind of serious relationship, having found the lesbian "scene" to be somewhat uninteresting. At the first instance she struck me as being a very confident, eloquent, sophisticated and glamorous older woman – just my type in fact! As we became acquainted, it transpired that she not only owned a hotel, but was also an extremely competent business woman in other fields, including the arts, something dear to my own heart. This all succeeded in making me fall for her, hook, line and sinker, despite the fact that she was (seemingly) happily married to a toyboy who appeared to have made a career out of being a kept man.

Nevertheless, as we struck up a friendship, I indulged myself in romantic notions and sexual fantasies, carefully allowing all references to her husband and heterosexuality go right over my head. At this point, I saw her as a dynamic femme fatale, whom I'd had the good fortune to meet and it was not until I introduced her to a close friend, that I began to think that maybe there was something different about her. My friend, Mandy, on meeting Tracie for the first time and then having to listen to me ramble on and on about how wonderful she was, exclaimed "That's not a woman, it's a sex-change!"

Silence ensued as I stared, dumbfounded at Mandy. Panic-stricken thoughts began to whirl through my head, she couldn't be a sex-change! She was a beautiful, independent, successful woman, there was no way she could be, or could have ever been, a man! (which was how I perceived the notion of transsexualism, what little I knew of it, at that time). I denied Mandy's statement, both to her face and to myself.

However, from that moment on, my mind worked overtime. The trademark lyrics of the Harmony Hairspray advertisement launched themselves at my brain, relentlessly: "Is she, or isn't she?" I continued to socialise with Tracie, becoming closer to her as a friend. I kept wondering if she was transsexual or not, out of curiosity than anything else. I was relating to her as I would another woman and I knew that even if I discovered her to be transsexual, it would not have a negative effect on our friendship.

It was not until she introduced me to a friend of hers, Maz, who described herself as a preoperative transsexual, that I finally decided to broach the subject with Tracie. We were sitting in Hyde Park one summer afternoon and found ourselves immersed in a discussion on gender. At some point in the debate, I could contain myself no longer and said that she should know how men operate as she used to be one, didn't she? Her immediate response was that she had never been a man. I then confessed that Maz had told me that she was a sex-change, but that she (Tracie) did not want me to know.

From this point on, the barriers came down. Once she realised that I did not have a problem with the notion of transsexuality, she allowed my questions to flow freely and any preconceptions I had previously were soon dispersed. I learned that she had been diagnosed as a classic transsexual at the age of eleven and had lived as a woman from the age of fifteen when she started taking hormones, having had rhinoplasty, breast augmentation and gender reaffirment surgery by the age of twenty two. So, although she had been born with the body of a biological male, she had never actually "been a man", and I had no problems in accepting her as another woman.

She has led an extremely colourful and varied life, at times painful and depressing, but it has made her a strong, versatile, intelligent, determined person. After about a year and a half into our friendship, her marriage having broken up, she finally succumbed to my persistent attempts to seduce her. I finally found the special woman I had been hoping to meet in all my time on the lesbian and gay scene. As time goes on, we continue to fall more and more in love with each other.

Sarah (partner of mascusexual)

In the fifteen years that I and my transsexual partner have been together, there have been many times when we have both wished that he was not transsexual. The rift with my parents as a result of this has been a hard burden to carry. Although my mother is mostly reconciled to the situation now, and my father, all these years later appears to be thawing. It would be nice not to always feel there is a secret which needs to be disclosed before friendships can progress. And there are times I long not to feel the anxiety that precedes this disclosure.

We wish we need not have had to suffer the misery of Stephen's loss of a much enjoyed job as a result of the situation. And that we might have escaped the grief and humiliation of being refused fertility treatment because we were not a suitable case. And I do get heartily bored of fielding inquiries about our sex life, since it appears that once penetration is not feasible, the imagination of the average heterosexual draws a blank. Yes, of course, there are many times I have wished Stephen was "normal" and that we had an "ordinary" relationship. But do I?

You see, we have had to examine ourselves and our relationship and we had to make it worth the fight. Our relationship has to be the best to compensate for the hassle. Since we have to suffer the aggravation of living with transsexuality, we live with it not against it. We are not going to hide away, pretending that we have some different history, too ashamed of ourselves and our relationship to tell the truth.

By not being afraid of losing friends as a result of being open with them, we have never lost a friend and have only closer friendships, since they are not hindered by skeletons in cupboards. And most people feel honoured that we regard them in high enough esteem to entrust them with this knowledge.

There have been many occasions when it has been fun to turn someone's reality upside down by announcing that one's partner has had a sex change. Of all the ghastly secrets which they have thought we would reveal, that one has not entered upon their consciousness. (Although it has to be admitted that the fact that we once owned and ran a hardware shop usually causes much greater amazement).

We have had the opportunity to have a much more interesting life than most. We have had the chance to be on television, on radio, interviewed for magazines. In fact, we dined out for years on the experiences which followed our first appearance on television. The trucker who recognised us and gave his vote of confidence, the pub landlady who offered us drinks and told us how wonderful we were! The letter in the "Radio Times" said the same. In fact, we began to see ourselves as special, not abnormal.

If it were not that Stephen was transsexual, he would not regularly attend conferences all over the world which discuss various aspects of transsexuality. We would not be off to Strasbourg, trying to improve the rights of transsexuals in this country.

Most of all, despite all our wishes, I look at our children and I know that had Stephen not been transsexual, we would not have had these children and I don't want to love any other children. And if Stephen had not been transsexual, he would not have been him and I don't want to love any other man.

Ida (Tracie's mother)

My youngest child when born was my son, but is now my daughter and has been for the past nineteen years. I was thirty nine years old when I realised my son, who was then eight years old was acting differently. At nine years old he ran away from home and was missing for five days, what a worry that was. When he was found, he was disguised as a woman, dressed in my clothes, which I did not know were missing. I was quite upset at the time and could not see or think of any reason why he had done this. Our relationship as parent and child got very strained, he got very much out of hand and was determined to do the things he wanted to do. It was painfully hard to cope, I had to call in the children's inspector and he called the doctor.

May I add that his father was being treated for a mental illness, so I was trying to cope with that also. The children's inspector and the doctor turned out to be good friends and a good support to me throughout those bad times. The doctor suggested he would like to take my son to London to see a specialist. He was now ten years old, so we put the suggestion to my son and he really wanted to make this visit. The doctor collected him on his day off, took him to London and back home again.

The specialist said he would see him when he was older to see if he would grow out of it, so the visits continued. My doctor spent a lot of time explaining to me how people get born with different organs inside them, I was surprised how many ways people are trapped in their own bodies. I learnt a lot from him as he was specialising in this subject.

When my child informed me, some years later that she was in hospital and had had the operation, I went to London to see her. It was quite a strange feeling, she was now my daughter instead of my son, but I was relieved to see she was all right. Obviously I felt cheated out of a relationship that could have been, but that has gone and one has to deal with what is here now and in the future. I cannot say this has changed me as a person, though I have to be on my guard a lot, when I see things going wrong. I want to offer a bit of advice, but it's rarely accepted. I suppose being a transsexual, they like to think they are making the right decision, but we all learn by our mistakes.

My friends and relations accept my daughter as she is, a person and is made welcome. One of her brothers doesn't accept it, the other one often enquires about her, but she doesn't get on with him. Being their mother puts me in the middle of the cross fire, all I want is my family to be friends with one another, then I can end my days happy. I accept my daughter as a transsexual, as that is what she wanted, to bring some peace into her life. I have asked her if she has ever regretted it and she definitely has not.

I would advise any mother faced with this situation to see it through, the child needs you. The child will hurt you, reject you and think people on the outside are better than you, though they all need friends and need space. But the love, friendship and help they need when in trouble, is their mother.

Marion (Vicky's mother)

Martin was born on 28th March 1959 and I was over the moon to have a baby son, as I already had a five and a half year old daughter who was just as delighted with her baby brother. Martin started primary school when he was five years old and fitted in well, although he liked the company of girls rather than boys. He enjoyed dressing up in frilly petticoats and my sister's high heeled shoes when we went for visits.

When Martin went into the Juniors at school, I noticed that he still continued to prefer to play with the girls. He would never go to games or play football with the boys, instead he would stay in the playground and participate in whatever the girls were doing. Just before Martin was eleven I took him to the hospital to see a child psychologist as his headmistress at school had said that Martin was very feminine – something which I was already well aware of! I was told by the hospital that Martin was a normal healthy boy who just happened to prefer the company of girls because they were not rough. He had a very unhappy time at secondary school because he was very gentle and sensitive – the other boys called him "poof" and other names.

On Martin's sixteenth birthday he had a lot of birthday cards from friends - all from male friends. I mentioned this to him and he looked at me and said "Mum, I've got something to tell you". I answered before he could say anything else, "I already know that you're gay". We cuddled one another and shed a few tears of relief and I will never forget what he said next, "Mum, I won't have to lie to you anymore". Family and friends were very understanding and supportive to Martin.

Over the next few years Martin felt increasingly more that he was a woman, cruelly trapped in a man's body and he also felt that it would be impossible and unbearable to carry on with life like this. Eventually, Martin went into hospital to have a sex change operation and came home the daughter I knew I should have had a long time earlier. None of the family or myself feel cheated in any way, because Martin became Vicky and she is still the same person we have always loved. Only now, since becoming Vicky, can she really be happy in herself and enjoy life as the woman she always knew she should have been.

Anna (Danielle's sister)

My original relationship with the transsexual was that of my brother, David. Now she is my sister, Danielle. I was twenty five when I first knew of her transsexuality, although I had always known she was different, but did not know how exactly.

My reaction was one of relief that at last it all made sense. I was happy that she had finally figured out what was obviously causing her so much pain and confusion all her life. I couldn't work out why I had not thought of it before. Our relationship then grew stronger again and trust that had been lost was restored. We could once again share things with one another. She stopped shutting me out and I stopped feeling guilty for not understanding what was happening to her. Danielle and I have always had more of a sisterly relationship anyway, so there has been little change in our relationship.

I coped by asking questions, reading books and talking to people. Knowing the facts is the best way of coping with anything, so I have had no problem with accepting Danielle's situation. I suppose the most support I had was from my friend, Jackie. I didn't feel any need for support really, so I didn't look for it, I don't think it would have made any difference in my case. I would say the only real effect it has had on my life is that I have seen a side of life that I would otherwise have been unaware of. It has made me more broad minded about life and accepting that people can be different, we don't all need to be the same. Whether I regret anything or not is unimportant, the important thing is that Danielle does not regret any decisions she has made about who she is.

The general reaction towards Danielle has been one of accepting interest with an undertone of amazed amusement. On one occasion at a family gathering she walked in unexpectedly, the family busy chatting when she appeared. Initially silence fell and mouths dropped open wide. Reactions were mixed, but on the whole they were accepting and interested in what she was doing. Well, it gave them all something a bit more interesting to talk about.

When the day of the operation came around, I had mixed feelings. I was happy for Danielle, but I couldn't help wondering if she was doing the right thing, until I saw her at the clinic after the operation. She never looked happier and I knew then that she had the made the right decision. As far as I am aware she received excellent mental and physical care and I believe she is most happy with the results.

Danielle's my sister, sometimes I love her, sometimes I hate her. She drives me nuts, but I'll always care about her. I worry about her because even though she has overcome so much, she has and always will have so much more to overcome. Life for her has become better, but it will always be hard.

Peter (father of mascusexual) – a sad story
I doubt whether my contribution will be acceptable for your publication, but I am compelled to write to you regardless. I found out about your forthcoming book from my wife who informed me that our daughter was going to contribute her story to it. My first reaction was anger - that my daughter should want to go public with her condition and I say "her" because as far as I am concerned, my wife gave birth to a daughter and I find the idea that she now thinks of herself as a man both preposterous and disturbing. Eight years ago when she was twenty two years old, Anne told her mother and myself that she was in a homosexual relationship with another woman. I found this very difficult to come to terms with, because as a Christian, this kind of thing is against the sanctity of the church and as a professor of theology it is necessary for me to retain a certain respectability and morality.

I have had little contact with my daughter since this time. My wife meets with her periodically outside of our home. She has done well for herself both academically and career wise and part of me is proud of her for this. I am only sad that she chose to live an immoral lifestyle, thereby ensuring my exclusion from it.

Now I am horrified to discover that my daughter believes herself to be a man. My wife arrived home extremely distraught one evening after a meeting with her. My daughter had told her that she had always felt that she should have been a boy and had now come to the realisation that this was her true self. To this end, she had begun taking male hormones and intended to undergo breast removal and a hysterectomy. I was shocked, to say the very least, at this revelation, and seeing my wife's terrible distress, I decided to meet with my daughter for the first time in eight years.

I had an appointment to meet at her house in Lincolnshire one afternoon. As I waited apprehensively at the front door, nothing could have prepared me for the unfortunate sight before me. Someone opened the door, half smiled and said "Hello dad". All I could do was stare in stunned horror. This person was not my daughter. This person had the voice of a man, a small beard and cropped hair. The last image I had of my daughter was just before she had revealed her homosexual tendencies to us. She was such a pretty girl with shoulder length brown hair and a sweet smile. I always thought that she would go to university and get her degree, get a good job and then marry. I never dreamed that something as dreadful as this could possibly happen to a child of mine.

I refused to go inside and left immediately, saying nothing to the person who was, once upon a time, my daughter. I cannot comprehend or condone what she has done to herself. There is a divine order in which we are all created and I believe it to be utterly wrong to defy this order. My wife prays for my daughter's soul. As far as I am concerned, my daughter is dead, I have no child.

I believe your book is intended to help people who wish to change and mutilate themselves like this. I am writing to express my abhorrence at such sacrilege of the human body. I only hope that in reading this story others planning to follow this path will be deterred.

Michael (brother of a femisexual)

At seven, my older brother, Patrick and I went to live with our aunt and uncle by the seaside. This was not through choice, but because our mum and dad were always so busy over in Hong Kong. Patrick or Patsie as he liked to be called is just two years older than me, but even then, it was like having a big, bossy, older sister. He was never one for playing rugby or cricket with the other boys, but spent a lot of time by the sea, lazily reading me stories from all his Enid Blyton books. Wherever Patsie went, I was never far behind.

At eleven I was sent off to school and never understood why Patsie stayed with my aunt and uncle attending the small village school, although it dawned on me little by little each time I came home that Patsie was absolutely nothing like any of the other brothers that the boys at school had. In fact, as the swinging sixties arrived, Patsie and flower power turned into something like no other relative of anyone I ever knew. As a hairdresser, Patsie just got away with being Patsie and people seemed to avoid the question of which or what sex my sibling had turned out to be.

When I was sixteen I came home to find my mother and father back from Hong Kong and auntie's house had turned into a war zone of insults, innuendoes and plain rudeness. I couldn't understand why mum and dad could leave us for so many years and then on arriving home do nothing but heckle Patsie like hags before the guillotine. When he moved to London suddenly I had a sister and no-one at the place Patsie worked had any idea about her past. I must admit for a few years it was precarious dashing between my parents and Patsie, changing to the correct pronouns appropriate to the company.

I've got to say, my sister's a hoot, by far one of the best things that ever happened to me. When she went to Casablanca to be operated on, I went with her. When I was married and both my children were born, Patsie was there. My wife adores her and I have no idea what it would be like to have had an older brother all my life, but it's been super fun to have a sister who turned out to be such a lovely person.

Mum and dad came round eventually and just before he died, my father became closer to Patsie than he had to any of us. I can't say I've been that keen on the first two chaps she lived with, but now she lives with an old school chum of mine, selling antiques on the coast in the South of France.

He's a nice chap really, and I think he's terribly lucky to have a partner so truly sweet as my dear sister.

Jane (friend of several mascusexuals)

When I was sixteen, I abruptly became aware of transsexuals and reacted appallingly! To elaborate, I was sitting at a table on a Retreat, waiting for dinner. Tables were organised such that one was plucked from the bosom of one's friends and thrust amongst strangers, in order to "meet people". The person I "met" was Andrew. Upon his enquiry about where I went to school, I informed him it was a girls' Grammar School. He announced that he went to a similar school. There followed the most confusing interaction, at complete cross purposes, in which I insisted that he must be mistaken. When he explained that he'd been a girl at the time, I held this revelation in complete disbelief.

Nonetheless, I thought it was the most terribly exciting Retreat I'd ever been on and immediately after the meal, rushed off with all the discretion and tact of a sixteen year old, to tell my companions. Andrew (then aged twenty-three) was with several friends, another of whom, James was also transsexual. After meeting them I returned to my former companions to tell them I'd be occupied all evening. I recall saying "He (James) is completely mad. When I go back, he'll probably be standing on his head". To my astonishment and horror, when I returned, he was! I thought this much more interesting and bizarre than all the sex change stuff, which by that time, had paled into insignificance.

It never occurred to me that I should get support to cope with this revelation. I was slightly nervous telling my mum, but in fact she was extremely cool about it. When I told my dad, my little sister nipped any possible adverse reaction in the bud, by telling him it was so old fashioned to mind about "sex exchanges". He was so desperate to appear trendy that he didn't dare say anything negative.

During the first meal at the Retreat, I'd had a lengthy

discussion with Andrew about transsexualism and sexuality. Why, I asked, did he not just become a lesbian? Furthermore, I thought it was a real cop out, in terms of feminism, to want to be a man, instead of fighting for equality as a woman. This raised for me, two crucial points. Transsexuality has nothing to do with sexual orientation and nothing to do with sexual politics.

After fifteen years, James, Andrew and I remain friends and still live together with Andrew's partner and our other friends. It's difficult to say how knowing my friends are transsexual has changed our relationship, as I have never known them as anything else. I find it hard to conceptualise that they were both born physically female, the notion is ludicrous and virtually impossible to square with the two men I've known for years. That they should have not taken the course they did is unthinkable. Because of that, it has probably been hard sometimes, to remember that the rest of the world doesn't necessarily see it that way. I've probably tended to minimise or not realise the difficulties, insecurities and discrimination they face.

Their experience of professional care has, I would say, been mixed. My general impression is that health services' staff are often individually supportive, but that resources are rather scarce. Having to fight for treatment to rectify an intolerable situation is pretty distressing and requires a huge amount of assertion. I feel a lot of respect for my friends for being able to do that whilst being in such a vulnerable position. It's something I remember when feeling less than brave myself.

On reflection, I certainly don't feel that I've been cheated out of friendships with non-transsexuals. On the contrary, at the risk of sounding sentimental, I feel my life has been enriched. Mind you, I don't think it's quite the enlightening experience the church youth group had in mind when taking me on Retreat!

Bernie (friend of femisexual)
I shall never forget that evening when the Blanche to be

flounced into our bedroom, a dead fox casually thrown round her neck, and proclaimed she was going to have a sex change. It had been quite a few weeks since I had last seen her. Then, my memory is of someone uncomfortably dressed in a sombre dark suit sitting cross legged in the hallway, purposefully packing and unpacking the suitcase in front of him. We'd spent the day tripping, it's true, but I still had the feeling that something wasn't quite right! The Blanche I know now, more than twenty years later, is the same person, but I had no idea how different they would be on the outside.

Both my parents have met Blanche. They always ask how she is, knowing she's a transsexual, amazed that someone so strange can be doing so well and living life so fully. Too polite to ask where all the money comes from, but suspecting the worst, my father admires her business sense, my mother is overwhelmed by the complexity of it all. When my younger sister had her 21st birthday, Blanche came to the barbecue and met my Aunts and Uncles. They were from up North and to them gay people were still a novelty. Meeting Blanche was an event that I'm sure had them talking for many days after.

Blanche is someone I'm proud to know. Just as straight people seem to benefit from knowing gay people, I feel I've benefited from knowing Blanche. Everything she has she has had to fight for, including the body that was denied her at birth. For most of us, our lives are full of assumptions, taking the things we have for granted. Gender is the most fundamental divisor of humanity; dividing into either male or female. Transsexuals have to deal with conflict at the most primitive level.

I was fortunate in that when I came out being gay was fashionable. For me, when Blanche announced her sex change, being transsexual was unheard of. A novelty, yes, and definitely a bit drastic. What if you changed your mind after the operation? But then I didn't realise, Blanche never had any intention of changing her mind. We'd never talked about changing sex, never sat up all night and had long meaningful conversations. It just happened. A bit unusual, granted, but for a young gay boy like me who had only recently come out, it was just one of the many queer events going on in my life, events that my straight, catholic upbringing had failed to prepare me for. How could I ever possibly imagine what it was be like to have a physical gender and a spiritual gender that didn't match up?

Blanche is someone I know, a friend like any other friend. She has no special privileges, no immunity from criticism, no special power. But she is a special person. Is it because she's transsexual? Not really. That ceased to be an issue many years ago. Would Blanche be the same person if she wasn't transsexual? Stupid question. How could you ever know?

Afterword

Finding a cure

The lamentable question of finding a cure, will be conceived differently from each and every individual's point of view. Normality, to a transsexual, bears little relevance to what is considered to be normality to a heterosexual, homosexual or even an omnisexual hamster. The general equation of normality is arrived at by a quantitative analysis of the masses, resulting in the dominance of a majority group, not necessarily in excess of the greater half.

Why do we even consider that the cure for transsexuality might bring a relief, equal to the pleasure of heterosexuality? Generally, most transsexuals inform us that they would not wish their state of being upon their worst enemy. This indicates the profound level of distress felt by those experiencing this condition. At the moment, it seems the most effective way to treat transsexuals is with surgery and hormone therapy. This is the best that the West has come up with so far, as a cure for transsexual Gender Dysphoria, eliminating the dysphoria leaving the client cosmetically attired to come in line with their own perception of themselves.

As the science of psycho-sexual behavioural genetics may, one day, be a fully fledged reality, then we might be able to look forward to choosing the sex, sexuality and gender of our children. Further to this, it might be possible to change the genetic ingredients during the course of the human life itself. Offer anyone a pill to change their sexual condition at will and the curiosity of the mind would prompt the intelligent human to explore, uninhibited.

Whether there is a prenatal or postnatal formulation of the transsexual being is only a matter that science will undoubtedly reveal in time. Its relevance to those who are presently living out their lives in this condition is mainly with the scientific implication that might eventually influence governments through the world to discontinue legal persecution.

Appendix A

Trans-Diversity

Transgenderists

A group of men attempt to attain a state of permanent prefemisexuality. They are not to be, at any time, confused with complisexuals. They have no desire for gender reaffirment operations and go under the label of transgenderist, living as women socially and taking hormones to feminise their appearance. Some even undergo breast and other surgeries including electrolysis in order to maximise their feminine aura, but at no time do they wish to be women. Homosexual, bisexual or heterosexual orientation may be present and they find the very idea of losing their male genitalia abhorrent. They do not want to be considered transsexual and have no desire to be female, but seem quite happy to live in a state of permanent prefemisexuality, which is self induced. To call them transvestites would be quite an anachronism, but to associate them with complisexuals would be quite inappropriate.

There are also women who are transgenderists, altering their bodies to appear socially to be men. They take hormones and may even undergo surgery to masculinise themselves. They do not wish to become men, only the masculine version of their female selves. Again, it would be wrong to classify these individuals as transsexuals, because they are happy to be and remain women. There are often raging debates that go on within the trans-everything community, accusing transsexuals of being elitist when attempting to define themselves separately from transgenderists. This does not mean that transsexuals deny the right for transgenderists to define themselves, whatever that self definition may be. There is a fight for

172

transgenderists to be recognised as a sub group in their own right. Some of them may wish not to be pushed into identifying as either male or female and some of them may want to identify as both. With this particular sub group their sex is not the issue, but their gender.

The static lines between categories of sex, sexuality and gender can be and often are fluid for people who have a strong identity of which group they belong to. For some transgenderists these fluid borders fluctutate and may even be semi-permanently or permanently mobile. Some transgenderists can be people who may have previously gone along the pre-complisexual route, but have decided, for some reason, to arrest their passage along that continuum and remain in a transgenderist identity. Although they may appear to be in a physical state of pre-femisexuality or mascusexuality, these people do not consider themselves identified with their opposite birth biological sex.

The transgenderist banner is often applied inaccurately to cover transsexuals, transvestites and transgenderists. It would be better to reserve the term, "transgenderist" for this particular special sub-group.

In America a couple both applied for sex reaffirment procedure at different clinics. The fact that they were partners went undiscovered for two years until a questionnaire coincidentally revealed the connection between them. As far as we know, they both went ahead with treatment.

We heard of a case of identical twin girls who both grew up and applied for sex reaffirment surgery together. They are now living together quite happily as two brothers.

Reports have come out of China about attempted transplantation of ovaries and wombs, but so far no success stories.

At the end of the eighties, a scientist was trying to perfect a method for biological men to have babies. This was theoretically achieved by implanting a fertilised egg ectopically, attaching it to the large intestine and then removing the foetus before full term, through surgical Caesarean. When we consulted the head of a professional gynaecological association, he told us that the occasional occurrence of this in nature in biological females usually instigates an immediate abortion. The chances of survival for both the host and the child are virtually non-existent.

In Polynesia, the fafafines are a group of people who believe that every third child should be a girl. If a male child he is born, he will be raised as female.

One of the most unusual findings we came across, during our research, was made by Julianne Imperato-McGinley and her colleagues, reported in 1974. They found an unusual phenomenon of pseudo-hermaphrodites, in the village of Salinas, in the Dominican Republic. A sum total of thirty three persons were located, all of whom seemed to have developed their condition, due to a deficiency of the enzyme, 5-alpha reductase. The enzyme is required in the prenatal period, to convert testosterone into a stronger androgen, dihydrotestosterone.

The male children, who lack this enzyme have testes, but do not have normal external genitalia. At birth, these individuals were labelled as girls, but during puberty, a penis became more evident, causing them to be known as "penis at twelve" children. On initial examination at birth, the testes looked like part of the labia mass and the penis, due to its lack of development, appeared to be a clitoris. During puberty, suddenly, the children's voices deepened and the penises grew and became sexually functional.

Of the thirty three individuals, nineteen had been raised as girls until puberty, when their bodies had changed in a masculine direction. One of the remainder changed his identity to male, but remained in a female work role.

Gender reassignment was sought by only one singular individual, who continued to identify as female.

Appendix B

Groups and Organisations

USA
INTERNATIONAL CONFERENCE ON TRANSGENDER LAW AND EMPLOYMENT POLICY, INC.
AMERICAN LAWYER (TRANSSEXUAL) SHE JUST LOVES A COURTROOM FIGHT, (ONE FORMIDABLE LADY)
PHYLLIS RANDOLPH FRYE.
5707 FIRENZA STREET,
HOUSTON, TEXAS 77035-5515, USA
TEL 713/723-8368
FAX   7231800

TRANSGENDERNATION.
AMERICAN TRANSSEXUAL LIBERATION GROUP
(HAVE A LOOK ON THE INTERNET FOR THEM)

(FOR PROFESSIONALS DEALING IN THE BUSINESS)
THE HARRY BENJAMIN INTERNATIONAL GENDER DYSPHORIA ASSOCIATION INC.
PO BOX 1718
SONOMA CA 95476
USA
TEL.(707)938-2871
FAX.(707)938-2871

INTERSEX SOCIETY OF NORTH AMERICA (ISNA)
PO BOX 31 791
SAN FRANCISCO
CALIFORNIA 94 131
USA

UNIVERSITY OF MICHIGAN MEDICAL CENTRE
DEPT. OF FAMILY PRACTICE
1018 FULLER STREET
ANN ARBOR
MICHIGAN 48109-0708
USA

PROGRAMME IN HUMAN SEXUALITY
DEPT. OF FAMILY PRACTICE & COMMUNITY HEALTH MEDICAL SCHOOL
UNIVERSITY OF MINNESOTA
1300 SOUTH 2ND STREET
SUITE 180
MINNEAPOLIS
MN 55454

CANADA
GENDER IDENTITY CLINIC CLARKE INSTITUTE OF PSYCHIATRY
250 COLLEGE ST
TORONTO
ONTARIO
CANADA
M5T 1R8

GENDER DYSPHORIA CLINIC
VANCOUVER GENERAL HOSPITAL
715 WEST 12TH AVENUE
VANCOUVER
BRITISH COLUMBIA
CANADA
V5Z 1M9

Appendix B

**TRANSSEXUAL SUPPORT GROUP
(DR. ANGELA WENSLEY)**
14905 32ND AVENUE
WHITE ROCK
BRITISH COLUMBIA
CANADA
VP4 1A4

ENGLAND
THE BEAUMONT TRUST
BM CHARITY
LONDON WCIN 3XX
HELPLINE TUESDAY AND
THURSDAY EVENING FROM 7PM
TO 11PM 071 730 7453

THE GENDER TRUST
BM GENTRUST
LONDON WC1N 3XX
SUPPORT NETWORK FOR
TRANSSEXUALS, TRANSVESTITES
AND TRANSGENDERED PEOPLE

FTM
BM NETWORK
LONDON
WC1N 3XX
SUPPORT NETWORK FOR FEMALE
TO MALE TRANSSEXUALS

PRESS FOR CHANGE
BM NETWORK
LONDON
WC1N 3XX

**VAGINOPLASTY NETWORK
(SOUTH)**
C/O MS HILARY EVERETT
GYNAECOLOGY SOCIAL WORKER
SOCIAL SERVICES DEPT
ST BARTHOLOMEW'S HOSPITAL
WEST SMITHFIELD
LONDON EC1A 7BE

**VAGINOPLASTY NETWORK
(NORTH)**
C/O MS SHEILA NAISH
ROYD WELL COUNSELLING
35 ROYD TERRACE
HEBDEN BRIDGE
WEST YORKSHIRE HX7 7BT

AIS SUPPORT GROUP (ALIAS)
C/O MS JACKIE BURROWS
2 SHIRBURN AVENUE
MANSFIELD
NOTTS. NG18 2BY

MERMAIDS
BM MERMAIDS
LONDON
WC1N 3XX
SUPPORT GROUP FOR FAMILIES
AND FRIENDS OF TRANSSEXUAL
CHILDREN AND ADOLESCENTS

SCOTLAND
CROSSLYNX TV/TS GROUP
C/O SLGS
POB 38
GLASGOW
SCOTLAND
G2 2QF

IRELAND
BELFAST BUTTERFLY CLUB
PO BOX 210
BELFAST
BT1 1BG
NORTHERN IRELAND

TRANSGENDER ARCHIVES
C/O DR RICHARD EKINS
UNIVERSITY OF ULSTER
COLERAINE
COUNTY LONDONDERRY
NORTHERN IRELAND

FRANCE
ASSOCIATION BEAUMONT
CONTINENTALE
C/O GABY LINSIG
2 RUE DES CHARPENTIERS
68270 WITTENHEIM
FRANCE

C.A.R.I.T.I.G
(CENTRE FOR HELP, RESEARCH
AND INFORMATION ON
TRANSSEXUALITY AND SEXUAL
IDENTITY)
PO BOX 17 .22
75810 PARIS CEDEX 17
FRANCE

SWITZERLAND
KONTAKTFORUM FEMME
TRAVESTIE
POSTFACH 6788
CH8023 ZURICH
SWITZERLAND

NETHERLANDS
GENDERTEAM AMSTERDAM
DEPT.
ENDOCRINOLOGY / ANDROLOGY
FREE UNIVERSITY HOSPITAL
PO BOX 7057
1007 MB
AMSTERDAM
NETHERLANDS

HUMANITS CONSULTING HOUR
FOR FAMILY-MEMBERS OF
TRANSSEXUALS
MRS. GERMAINE NIJSTEN
HUMANIST COUNSELLOR
MONDAY 2-5 PM
NATIONAL BUREAU HUMANITAS
STARPHATISTRAAT 4,
POSTBOX 71, 1000 AB AMSTERDAM,
HOLLAND.
TEL.O2O 62 62 445

NEDERLANDSEVERENIGING
HUMANTITAS
PO BOX 71
1000 AB AMSTERDAM
NETHERLANDS

GERMANY
TRANSIDENTITÄS
POSTFACH 101046
6050 OFFENBACH
GERMANY
TEL. 069 8001008

INTERSEX SUPPORT NETWORK
CENTRAL EUROPE (ISSNCE)
C/O HEIKE SUSANNE SPREITZER,
M.A.
RHEINSTRAUSSE 2
50 676 K÷LN
GERMANY

BUNDESINITIATIVE DER
TRANSSEXUELLEN BdT)
GESCHƒFTSSTELLE, C/O UWE G.
KLAASSEN
MINDENER STRASSE 15
10589 BERLIN
GERMANY

FINLAND
SETA
PO BOX 55
SF-00531
HELSINKI
FINLAND

TURKEY
TRAVESTY / TRANSSEXUALLE
C/O DEMET DEMIR
LAO 176/D.S.
KULTUR JE SANAT
SIRASELVILER
TAKSIM
ISTANBUL
TURKEY
DO NOT MENTION NAME OF
GROUP ON ENVELOPE.

AUSTRALIA
GENTRUST INFORMATION LINE
0305 269222 BEFORE 10PM
THE GENDER CENTRE (GENDER ISSUES)
75 MORGAN STREET,(PO BOX 266)
PETERSHAM NSW 2089
AUSTRALIA
TEL.569 2366 FAX.569 1176
MONDAY-FRIDAY 10AM-5.30PM

NEW ZEALAND
NEW ZEALAND GENDER DYSPHORIA FOUNDATION
PO BOX 2827
AUCKLAND
NEW ZEALAND

PAKISTAN
KHUSRA OF PAKISTAN
MUHAMID ASLAM KHUSRA
EX-CANDIDATE
PF-34 ABBOTABAD
C/O HOCKEY STADIUM
ABBOTABAD
PAKISTAN
05921 6158/2858

EASTERN EUROPEAN REPUBLICS
GENDER TRANSIENT AFFINITY OF LATVIA
ELGA REMES, DIRECTOR
JURMALA
-15
PO BOX 17
2015 LV
LATVIA

RUSSIA
ICE AND FIRE, MOSCOW
678190 AIHAL
YAKUTIA
GAGARINA STR NO 28
FLAT NO 3
RUSSIA
DO NOT MENTION NAME OF GROUP OR TITLE ON ENVELOPE.

JAPAN
ELIZABETH CLUB
5-32-18 KAMEIDO
KOTO-KU
TOKYO 136
JAPAN
TEL. 03-3683-6092

SOUTH AFRICA
THE PHOENIX SOCIETY HELPLINE
BOX 6433
PAROW-EAST 7500
SOUTH AFRICA

WEST AFRICA
TRANSFORMATION SECOND SELF
JANE ENUNEKU
KM 4 IDIROKO ROAD
PO BOX 1006
OTA
OGUN STATE
NIGERIA
WEST AFRICA

STICHTING EDE
ONLY FOR FEMALE- TO MALE TRANSSEXUALS (PREFEMISEXUAL/FEMISEXUALS)
BENNEKEMSEWEG 160
6871 KJ RENKEM
TEL. 083 73-18 89 0
THE FOUNDATION IS A SELF HELP GROUP.
THE EDE FOUNDATION PROMOTES THE INTEREST OF (F-M) TRANSSEXUALS AND AIMS TO PROVIDE A SERVICE OF HELP BOTH EMOTIONALLY AND PRACTICALLY. AT THE SAME TIME IT ORGANISES SOCIAL EVENTS AND DISCUSSION GROUPS.

Appendix C

Conferences

THE CONFERENCE E.N.P.T.

A conference for the European Network of Professionals on Transsexualism was held at Manchester University on August 31st to September 2nd 1994. This was the second conference of its kind. The chairman of the conference was Professor Louis Gooren, internist, from Amsterdam. The conference secretariat was Mr Jos Megens from the department of endocrinology and andrology from the Free University Hospital (AZVU) Amsterdam, Holland.

As usual, at any conference on transsexualism the stage was taken mainly by a proliferation of psychiatrists and clinical psychologists. No geneticists made a presentation and only the odd reference was made to the genetic fundamentals that may one day, form the basis of transsexual diagnosis. Many worthy and compassionate presentations were made concerning the transsexual experience and culture, but most of the information was correlated by non transsexual candidates, with little regard for the real political and legal issues that fail to protect this vulnerable, unprotected sector of society. The only complisexual at the conference, who had managed to secure a job in a gender identity clinic, was Maxine Peterson MA from Toronto, Canada.

GENDY'S 94

This conference immediately followed the E.N.P.T. at Hulme Hall, Manchester University and seemed to be for those who were presently gender dysphoric. Very few complisexuals attended, and Alice Purnell, the organiser, said how she would like to see more support from the no longer gender dysphoric transsexual community. Some experts in the field spoke, making it a most informative forum for those who were presently in treatment. Accommodation was available in the halls of the university and the very well organised Ms Purnell made it as much a social event as a symposium, an approach that many a clinician could learn from. She also saw it as a chance to network and to raise consciousness, as well as to aim for a high quality of care and follow-up for the gender dysphoric. It is also hoped that it would promote research and dispel some of the mythologies about gender identity conflict.

The event was unusual in that it had parallel symposiums for both femisexuals and mascusexuals.

GENDY'S 96

The Gendy's 96 conference was an even bigger event with over two hundred and thirty gender dysphoric and ex-gender dysphoric people attending the dinner and disco in the evening. According to Alice Purnell this was probably the largest gathering of the brothers and sisters in Europe.

Again on the Saturday were parallel symposiums for pre/femisexuals and pre/mascusexuals with masses of information and interesting topics. Amongst the speakers was a transsexual who herself is a surgeon and has survived the transition whilst still remaining in a high profile position. We know that while she is greatly respected as a surgeon she was, before the change in the European law (winter 96), terrified of losing her career.

Sporting his "Transsexual Menace" T-shirt was Dr. Stephen Whittle, a senior lecturer in law at Manchester University. This organisation, we believe, is an international group of people dedicated to attaining equal human rights for all trans-people.

At the conference Christine Burns made a plea for volunteers to help with lobbying political party conferences. Many people came forward and offered help in different ways for the fight for equal rights, but she emphasised that one can never have too many volunteers.

This event was indeed a healthy forum for the treatment and issues affecting the trans community and not all clinicians were in agreement, openly and publicly debating their different theories and applications.

XIV HARRY BENJAMIN INTERNATIONAL GENDER DYSPHORIA SYMPOSIUM.

The 1995 conference was held in a remote Bavarian monastery that now was equipped as a conference facility. It was suspected by many delegates that its inconvenient assembly far away from an airport was purposefully convened in order to preclude too many new theorists. However, this suspected plot failed, as the transsexual intellectuals turned up in numbers and proceeded to police the homogeneous multi discipline melting pot.

Amongst the coming together of surgeons, sociologists, psychologists, psychiatrists, psychotherapists, social workers, lawyers, endocrinologists, gynaecologists, urologists and a hypnotherapist were an even greater diversity of ...ologists, ...erapists and ...iatrists than was ever declared. The theoretical aetiologies and managements of transsexualism were presented by representatives from more than twenty countries world wide.

Some of the presentations or works, philosophies and proposed developments were inspirational and others were mere crackpot. Amongst the former, Professor Gooren and his team from Holland displayed a range of treatments, research projects and approaches, which the Dutch government provides for transsexuals, which are the envy of the world.

There were however some early twentieth century psycho-theorists who made presentations, of theoretical transsexual psychodynamics, that were merely figments of their own imaginations. In fact, amongst a profusion of cerebral systemic philosophies, it was a toss up, at times, on who was going to section who.

Dr. Montgomery of London complained that amongst

such a seminal meeting of minds, the plenary should be, by far, the most important slot. Alice Purnell, of the Gentrust, suggested that next time the commendation of the client group might be more appropriate rather the adoration of the dead Harry Benjamin. The French academia were notably absent – perhaps they had nothing to learn or were too busy with nuclear-physics.

In all, it is without doubt, one of the most important conferences, that is held, concerning the transsexual phenomenon. Perhaps, in the future however, it could widen its concepts of the transsexual or the transgendered in order to demarcate the boundaries of gender, sex and sexuality. Perhaps we all could?

The cross cultural conflicts of human behavioural expectations were profoundly apparent and language seemed such a small barrier to the preconceived concepts everyone had brought with them. Only by world events, such as this, can the accommodation of trans-anything come about.

One of the sad things about the conference, was that many of those present had taken their statistics from their own clinics alone. During the research of this book, it has become evident to us, that many of the gender dysphoric do not attend some of these authoritarian and inflexible institutions. Private medicine affords a lot of clients a great deal of choice to place their money where it is most respected. Academia, with its exclusive view of itself has here, once again, through its own gratification, missed the big picture.

The HBIGDA has openly admitted that a drastic reappraisal of its standards of care is needed and that its very members are amongst those who are flagrantly disregarding those guidelines. Due to cross-cultural, international differentials, it is very difficult for standards to be applied universally. However, the transsexual community strongly feels that the HBIGDA seems unable to grasp the concept that it is the clinicians who define transsexuality as a pathology. The patients themselves see the clinicians as a facility, which is often denied, as western medicine attempts, once again, to play God. There are also proposals being considered within this organisation to extend its caring guidelines beyond the purely transsexual issues to accommodate a wider spectrum of gender dysphoria.

Bibliography

ASHLEY, APRIL & FALLOWELL, DUNCAN
"April Ashley's Odyssey" London 1982 Cape.

BANDLER, RICHARD & GRINDER, JOHN
"The Structure of Magic" USA 1975 Science & Behaviour
Books Inc

BENJAMIN, HARRY
"The Transsexual Phenomenon" NY 1966 Julian Press

BORNSTEIN, KATE
"Gender Outlaw" NY & London 1994 Routledge.

BOCKTING, WALTER O. & COLEMAN, ELI, PHD,
(EDITORS)
**"Gender Dysphoria – Interdisciplinary Approaches in
Clinical Management"** NY 1993 Haworth Press.

BULLOUGH, VERN L. & BONNIE
"Cross Dressing, Sex and Gender" 1993
Philadelphia. University of Pennsylvania Press

COLLINS **English dictionary, third edition.** Harper
Collins London 1991.

COSSEY, CAROLINE
"My Story" London 1991 Faber and Faber.

COOK-DEEGAN, ROBERT
**"The Gene Wars. Science, Politics and the Human
Genome".** USA 1994 Norton.

COUNTY, JAYNE WITH RUPERT SMITH
"Man Enough to be a Woman" 1994 NY & London.
Serpent's Tail

COWELL, ROBERTA
"Roberta Cowell's Story" London 1954 Heinemann.

CUMMINGS, KATHERINE
"Katherine's Diary: The Story of a Transsexual"
Melbourne 1992 Heinemann.

ERICKSON, MILTON H. & ROSSI, ERNEST LAWRENCE
ROSSI,
"The February Man" 1989 New York Brunner/Mazel Inc.

FAUSTO-STERLING, ANNE
"Myths of Gender" USA 1985 Basic Books

FEINBERG, LESLIE
"Transgender Warriors" USA 1996 Beacon Books

GARBER, MARJORIE
"Vested Interests: cross-dressing and cultural anxiety
London 1992 Penguin.

GRAHAM, PHILLIP
"Child Psychiatry: A developmental approach". Oxford
NY Tokyo 1986 Oxford University Press.

GRANT, JULIA
"Just Julia" London 1994 Boxtree Ltd.

GRINDER, JOHN & BANDLER, RICHARD
"The Structure of Magic II" USA 1976 Science &
Behaviour Books inc

HEWITT, PAUL
"A Self-Made Man" London 1995 Headline Book Publishing.

Bibliography

HODGKINSON, LIZ
"Michael née Laura" London 1989 Columbus.

HODGKINSON, LIZ
"Bodyshock" London 1987,1991 Virgin.

JORGENSEN, CHRISTINE
"Christine Jorgensen: A personal autobiography
NY 1967 Bantam.

LEWINS, FRANK
"Transsexualism in Society" Australia 1995 MacMillan
Education Australia PTY Ltd.

MILLOT, CATHERINE
"Horsexe" USA 1990 Autonomedia Inc.

MORRIS, JAN
"Conundrum" London 1987 Penguin.

NATAF, ZACHARY
"Lesbians talk Transgender" London 1995 Scarlett Press

RAMSEY, GERALD, PhD
"Transsexuals" California 1996 The Crossing Press

RAYMOND, JANICE
"The Transsexual Empire" London 1980 The Women's
Press.

REES, MARK
"Dear Sir or Madam" London & NY 1996 Cassell

ROBBINS, ANTHONY
"Unlimited Power" London & NY 1986 Simon &
Schuster Ltd

ROSSI, ERNEST LAWRENCE
"The Psychobiology of Mind-Body Healing" NY &
London 1993 Norton

RUTHERFORD, ERICA
"Nine Lives" Canada 1993 Ragweed Press.

SMITH, TONY (Medical Editor)
**"British Medical Association Complete Family Health
Encyclopaedia"** 1994 London Dorling Kindersley Ltd.

SPAIN, DAPHNE
"Gendered Spaces" USA 1992 University of North
Carolina Press.

STOLLER, ROBERT J
**"Sex and Gender: on the development of masculinity
and femininity"** London 1968 Hogarth Press and Institute
of Psycho-analysis.

STUART, KIM ELIZABETH
"The Uninvited Dilemma" USA 1983 Metamorphous
Press.

SULLIVAN, LOUIS
"From Female to Male: The life of Jack Bee Garland"
Boston 1990 Alyson Publications Inc.

TAYLOR, TIMOTHY
"The PreHistory of Sex" London 1996 Fourth Estate Ltd

THOMPSON, RAYMOND
"What took you so long?" London 1995 Penguin

TRUDGILL, PETER,
**Sociolinguistics: An Introduction to Language and
Society** London 1983 Penguin.

WILDEBLOOD, PETER
"Against the Law" Middx. 1955 Penguin.

ZUCKER, KENNETH J & BRADLEY, SUSAN
"Gender Identity Disorder and Psychosexual Problems in Children and Adolescents" NY 1995 Guilford Press

PAPERS
"Psychomedical aspects of gender problems"
Abstract book of posters presented at the first meeting of a European Network of Professionals on Transsexualism. The Free University Gender team, Amsterdam April 18-20th 1993

Transsexualism, Medicine and Law
XXiiird Colloquy on European Law, Amsterdam April 14-16th 1993

"From peniplastis totalis to reassignment surgery of the external Genitalia in female to male transsexuals".
By J.Joris Hage.
Vu University Press
Vu Boekhandel/uitgeverij bv
De Boelelaan 1105
1081 hv Amsterdam, The Netherlands

"Memory Mechanisms" AMA Archives of Neurology and Psychiatry, 1952, vol. 67. by Wilder Penfield.

"Unfavourable Long-Term Results of Rectoisigmoid Neocolpopoiesis"
by J.Joris Hage, M.D, refaat B.Karim, M.D, Henk Asscheman, M.D, Ph.D, Elisabeth Bloemena, M.D, Ph.D, and Miguel A.Cuesta, M.D, Ph.D.
The Dept. of Plastic and Reconstructive Surgery, Andrology, Pathology and General Surgery at the Academic Hospital of the Free University 1994.

"Legal Responses To Transsexualism: Scientific Logic Versus Compassionate Flexibility In The U.S. and The U.K."
Louis H. Swartz, Ph.D, LL.M, R.N, State University of New York at Buffalo, School of Social Work. 1995.

"Transsexualism: The Current Medical Viewpoint"
Dr. Russell Reid, Hillingdon Hospital, London, Dr. Domenico de Cegli, Tavistock Clinic, Mr. James Dalrymple, London Bridge Hospital, Professor Louis Gooren, University of Amsterdam, Dr Richard Green, Gender Identity Clinic, Charing Cross Hospital, Professor John Money, John Hopkins Hospital, USA . February 1995

Abstract Posters for the X1V Harry Benjamin International Gender Dysphoria Symposium.
The Harry Benjamin International Gender Dysphoria Association Inc, with
Department of Psychotherapy, Ulm University, Ulm, Germany.
Sept. 7-10th 1995.

Analysis of the CYP21B gene in female to male transsexual individuals by PCR-SSSP method.
R. Sachse, X. Shao, R. Krähner, G. Stalla, T. Mösler, J. Hensen.

A sex difference in the human brain and its relation to transsexuality
Jlang-Ning Zhou, Michel A. Hofman, Louis J. G. Gooren & Dick F. Swaab

SRY and Sex Determination In Mammals
Peter N. Goodfellow, Dept. of Genetics, University of Cambridge,
Robin Lovell-Badge, National Institute for Medical Research.
1995. Annual Reviews Inc.

Unnecessary Links between Transsexualism and Stress
Tracie O'Keefe
GemsNews 21
Newsletter published by The Gender Trust, BM Gentrust,
London WC1N 3XX.

**What is hypnotherapy and how can it help the
transsexual or transgendered individual**
Tracie O'Keefe
GemsNews 20

You can't tell by looking at them
Tracie O'Keefe
GemsNews 24

Three Weddings and a Gender Reassignment
Tracie O'Keefe
GemsNews 22

A Big Thank You to anyone even vaguely gay
Tracie O'Keefe
GemsNews 25

Observer Newspaper 15th September 1996.

VIDEOGRAPHY
**A CHANGE OF SEX PART ONE AND TWO –
JULIA GRANT STORY**
BBC1 1994

TAKING LIBERTIES – JOANNE'S STORY BBC1 1995

THE DAY THAT CHANGED MY LIFE BBC2 1995 –
MARK REES STORY.

THE DECISION – CHANNEL FOUR 1996 –
MASCUSEXUALS

FILMS
THE CHRISTINA JORGENSON STORY
ERPPER RAPPER 1970

SECOND SERVE
ANTHONY PAGE 1986

THE CRYING GAME
NEIL JORDAN 1994

DRESSED TO KILL
BRIAN DE PALMA 1980

THE SILENCE OF THE LAMBS
JONATHAN DEMME 1991

DOG DAY AFTERNOON
SIDNEY LUMET 1975

MYRA BRECKINRIDGE
MICHAEL SARNE 1970

I DON'T WANNA BE A BOY
ALEX BEHRENS NETHERLANDS 1995 -
(TRANSSEXUAL PROSTITUTES)

Further Reading

MAGAZINES
TRANSSISTERS.
(AMERICAN MAGAZINE OF TRANSSEXUAL
FEMINISM)
C/O DAVINA ANNE GABRIEL
4004 TROOST AVENUE
KANSAS CITY
MO 64110, USA

TAPESTRY (MAGAZINE)FOR PERSONS INTERESTED
IN SOME TRANSSEXUAL ISSUES.
IFGE BOX 367
WAYLAND, MA 01778, USA

GENDERTRASH
BOX #500-62
552 CHURCH ST
TORONTO
CANADA M4Y 2E3

**IN YOUR FACE – JOURNAL OF POLITICAL
ACTIVISM AGAINST GENDER OPPRESSION**
C/O RIKI ANNE WILCHINS
274 W.11TH ST #4R
NY
NY 10014, USA

JOURNAL OF GENDER STUDIES
OUTREACH INSTITUTE
405 WESTERN AVENUE, SUITE 345
SOUTH PORTLAND
ME 04106, USA

TRANSSEXUAL NEWS TELEGRAPH
41 SUTTER ST #1124
SAN FRANCISCO
CA 94104-4903, USA

POLARE. A MAGAZINE FOR PEOPLE WITH GENDER
ISSUES.
ADDRESS FOR CORRESPONDENCE
POLARE, PO BOX 226
PETERSHAM NSW 2O49
AUSTRALIA
TEL (02) 569-2366
FAX (02) 569-1176

RADICAL DEVIANCE
G&SA
BOX 8
ST MARY'S CENTRE
CORPORATION ROAD
MIDDLESBOROUGH
TS1 2RW

THE TRANNY GUIDE 1997
WAYOUT PUBLISHING COMPANY
PO BOX 70
ENFIELD EN1 2AE
ENGLAND

BOOKS
**TRANSVESTISM, TRANSSEXUALISM AND THE
LAW.**
BY MELANIE MCMULLAN & STEPHEN WHITTLE,
AVAILABLE FROM THE GENDER TRUST/THE
BEAUMONT SOC.
BM GENTRUST LONDON WC1N 3XX

TRANSSEXUALISM, TRANSGENDERISM AND GENDER DYSPHORIA
THE HANDBOOK OF THE GENDER TRUST (AS ABOVE).

HORMONES BY SHEILA KIRK, MD.
AVAILABLE FROM
IFGE PUBLICATIONS,
PO BOX 367, WAYLAND, MA.017780367
USA
TEL (617)899 2212
FAX (617)899 5703
ALSO AVAILABLE BY SAME AUTHOR;

HORMONES FOR FEMALE TO MALE TRANSSEXUALS
HORMONE TREATMENT FOR THE TRANSSEXUAL
THE EMPLOYER'S GUIDE TO GENDER TRANSITION

Professional Resources

TRACIE O'KEEFE B.A. ADV. DIP.THP.
(HYPNOTHERAPIST, PSYCHOTHERAPIST &
COUNSELLOR).
THE LONDON MEDICAL CENTRE
144 HARLEY STREET
LONDON
W1N 1AH
TEL. 0171 439 1995
FAX 0171 439 3536
E-MAIL katfox@easynet.co.uk
Member of British Register of Complementary
Practitioners
Member of National Council of Psychotherapists
Member of Hypnotherapy Register

THE GENDER IDENTITY CLINIC,
CHARING CROSS HOSPITAL,
LONDON
TEL.0181 846 1234
FAX. 0181 846 1133

FREE UNIVERSITY HOSPITAL(G I CLINIC)
DE BOELELAAN 1117
1008 AMSTERDAM
HOLLAND

A list of your local GI clinics may be obtained by
communicating with people in your locality on the internet,
from your doctor and from self help groups.

INTERNET AND WORLD WIDE WEB RESOURCES

TRANSGENDER FORUM (weekly E-zine)
http://www.tgforum.com

TRANSGENDER FORUM RESOURCE CENTER
http://www.tgfmall.com

TRANSGENDER FORUM COMMUNITY CENTER
http://www.transgender.org/tg/

TRANSMED REGISTRY (database for medical practitioners, therapists etc. who deal with the trans-community) http://www.maedata.com/transmed

AEGIS (American Educational Gender Information Service inc.). This is a non profit clearinghouse for information on transgender and transsexual issues. They maintain the National Transgender Library and Archive. At the time of press they have no web site only an FTP site at ftp://ftp.mindspring.com/users/aegis/ When it says User ID: anonymous and for Password: (your e-mail address). They also have electronic mailing lists, send e-mail to listserv@xconn.com;

FTM INTERNATIONAL http://www.ftm-intl.org/intro.html

GENDER TRUST UK http://www3.mistral.co.uk/gentrust

TRACIE O'KEEFE & KATRINA FOX (the authors) (http://easyweb.easynet.co.uk/~katfox/

Paper by Tracie O'Keefe

EXTENDING TRANSSEXUAL DIAGNOSIS
(Harry Benjamin Conference, Canada 1997)

I am Tracie O'Keefe, a clinical hypnotherapist and psychotherapist at the London Medical Centre, London, England. Not only am I a clinician who treats transsexuals but I am also a transsexual myself. I have blossomed as a person and a professional after having started to undergo treatment for gender dysphoria some thirty years ago. My considerations here are not only from a clinical point of view but also a consensus of opinions I have noted having had thirty years of living in and out of the transsexual community.

The use of language is as an important way of treating Gender Dysphoria and the Ex-Gender Dysphoric, as is the scalpel, hormones or cosmetic surgery. How we relate to others verbally, is not only through the descriptive pronoun or personal naming but also a public declaration of what that person's status is in society at large.

My name is Tracie, therefore my value as a human being equals whatever the user of my name sees, hears, and feels about me. When I say Tracie I am placing my own value upon myself. When others say my name Tracie, they are placing their value upon me. If I am called "she" then I am identified within our society as female but if I am called "he" then my whole value as a human being changes regardless of my culture of origin.

In the area of gender re-affirment treatment, it can be a minefield when someone misuses another person's pronoun, saying "she" when perhaps the client prefers "he" or vice versa. Indeed male and female are two distinctive ends of the reproductive sex continuum.

However, none of us as clinicians, surgeons or social

workers can actually change the sex of our clients, so to lead them to believe this on our part is total dishonesty. We cannot change biological males to females, or women to men. What our clients want, when they ask for a sex change, is for the clinician to help them re-affirm their believed sex.

The dictionary defines sex as a reproductive process and at present we cannot change the reproductive process of our clients, so therefore it is incorrect for us to label our clients as sex changes. There is no such thing as a sex change in the human equation.

Using the term sex change is offensive to many transsexuals, since it bestows biological expectations upon the patient that they cannot perform. It disempowers the ex-Gender Dysphoric because they feel they were never their original biological sex and do not want to have to live up to the biological expectations of their cosmetic sex.

The Terms M-F and F-M do not describe the transsexual experience for the majority of the transsexual population. We propose to offer you some logical linguistic extensions to the transsexual experience that can help you have greater choice in communicating with and describing your clients.

The linguistic surface structure of the phrases sex-change, the terms M-F and F-M, when examined closely reveal that such phrases are misnomers when applied to the transsexual experience. They are falsehoods that do not leave any of the users with the full satisfaction of descriptive language. Their deep root structure is in fact found to be a contradiction in terms. In order to allow the users of language describing the transsexual experience to feel more comfortable there needs to be new words, specific and special to that experience and not borrowed from the heterosexual bipolar model.

We are our language, and we become our descriptions just as new descriptions are sometimes needed to relate to new experiences.

Pansexual

To take into account the whole span across the sexes, genders, and sexualities.

Prefemisexual (transsexual)

A transsexual who is crossing the gender barriers from male to female, but has not yet undergone genital surgery.

Femisexual (transsexual)

A transsexual who crosses the gender barriers from male to female, having completed genital surgery.

Premascusexual (transsexual)

A transsexual who is crossing the gender barriers from female to male, but has not yet undergone genital surgery.

Mascusexual (transsexual)

A transsexual who has crossed the gender barriers from female to male, having had genital surgery.

Complisexual (transsexual) – either mascusexual or femisexual

One who has undergone the transsexual experience, now living in their desired gender role, having had genital surgery.

Primary Mascusexual/femisexual

One who knows from a very early age that they are the opposite gender to the body they have. These individuals find it impossible to live as their biological sex and begin to live as members of their believed gender from their teenage years.

Secondary Mascusexual/femisexual

One who discovers later in life that they are transsexual. These people may have known from an early age that they were not the gender that they outwardly appeared to be, but fought against the issue, often marrying and having children. In other words they manage to live and survive, although not necessarily happily so, as members of their biological sex

Transmen/Transwomen/Transperson

These are common language terms that have been used to describe those who live across the bipolar gender barrier to their original biological sex.

Paper by Tracie O'Keefe

TO LABEL OR NOT TO LABEL?

Here I am not presenting a fait accompli to say, "This is the way you should label your clients". I am not even saying for all clients this is right. I am simply offering a way out of the dilemma of having to associate clients with what might have been an offensive self image.

Being a femisexual myself, I know that I become very disturbed when the medical profession describes me as having once been male, for I plainly never have been. I, like all transsexuals were born somewhere in limbo land and spent a lifetime defining my own existence in the most comfortable way I could.

It is extremely insulting to me when someone describes me as once having been male, and I have nothing against males, I just never was one. The majority of transsexuals I have met feel the same as I do. If they had ever believed they were their original biological sex then they would have been unlikely to be in a position where they felt they had to claim their true identity.

Some people believe that more labels will only lead to a greater division in an already divided subculture. Others believe we should all be under the same banner to enforce the rights of all human beings, and so do I in a way. I believe we should allow our clients to express their experiences in using the fullness of language which they can define and claim the beneficial entitlements of those descriptions.

The emergence of a Trans-Fluid culture demonstrates that the old bipolar system of male and female simply cannot be applied to all of us. I hope you will consider seriously, in future, the way you are able to refer to your clients. Only by empowering the transsexual experience with extended logistic diagnosis are you able to empower those individuals to claim their right to be themselves. That is themselves not purely in relation to the exclusively rigid bipolar reproductive male and female experience.

Viva transfluidity, and learn from the gender adventurers who have a great deal to teach. Do not use

201

language to categorise your clients into a diagnostic criteria. Do not use language to secure your own understanding of your client's experience. Use language to empower, motivate, enrich, validate and appreciate the uniqueness of your clients' sense of well being.

I am Tracie, which equals a femisexual woman and a complisexual. I thank you.

We hope you have enjoyed our explorations and explanations of the world of transsexualism. Many of you may agree profoundly with some of our considerations and others will perhaps disagree with us on other points. If you have any comments, information or simply want to tell us how it is or was for you, please write to us at **Extraordinary People Press, Suite 412 Triumph House, 185 - 191 Regent Street, London W1R 7WB, England. Tel. 0171 734 3749. Fax. 0171 439 3536.**
E-Mail katfox@easynet.co.uk
Web site
http://easyweb.easynet.co.uk/~katfox/

Please note that any correspondence we may receive, we will take as an acknowledgement that we have permission to reproduce it in later publications.

Index

Abnormalities in pregnancy, 27
Acaults, 118
Acid skin peel, 65
Ashley, April, 105
Australia, 107
  Gender Centre, 76,177

Barrett, Dr. James, 69
Barry, Dr. James, 7
Behavioural training schools, 77
Benjamin, Harry, 2
  International Gender Dysphoria
  Association Inc., 126, 176
  XIV International Gender
  Dysphoria Symposium, 182-184
Beyer, Georgina, 111
Body concepts, 20
Bornstein, Kate, 116
Brain composure, 24
Brainwaves, 24
Breast augmentation, 60-63
Burns, Christine, 110, 181

Capsular contraction, 63
Careers, 95-97
Carlile, Alex, 109
Carr, Dr. Susan, 101
Causes of transsexualism
  *See Transsexualism, possible
  causes of*
Charing Cross Gender Identity
  Clinic, 196
Child abuse, incidence of in
  transsexual population, 45
Childlessness, 98-99
Children, 99
  and the law, 107-108
Chin reduction, 58
Christian church, 117
Chromosomal differentials, 28

Chromosome sexing, 34-36
Chronic Childlessness
  Syndrome, 98
Clitoplasty, 70
Collagen, 64
Colonoplasty, 73
Complications, 73-74
Complisexual, xxi
  management, 87-89
Cook-Deegan, Robert, 30
Corbett v *Corbett*
  See Ashley, April
Cornwall County Council, 112
Cossey, Caroline, 10, 91
  See also Tula
Cossey v *United Kingdom*, 92
Costing (of surgery), 75
Counselling, 78-79
Cowell, Roberta, 33
Cri du Chat Syndrome, 28
CYP21B gene, 31

Depilation, 77-78
Dermabrasion, 64
Dilation, 74
Dillon, Dr. Michael, 7
Diagnoses, bad, 44
Diagnosis, 33
Diagnostic criteria, 47
Disassociative disorders, 45-46
Down's Syndrome, 35
Dutch, the, 94

Ears, 58
Egypt, 107
Electrolysis,
  See Depilation
ENPT Conference, 180
Erickson, Milton, 81
Expected gender roles, 40-41

Index

Eye jobs
 See facelifts and eyejobs

Facelifts and eyejobs, 60
Facial implants, 58
Fat transfer, 64
Feminism,
 transsexualism and, 119-123
Femisexual, xxi
Femisexuality and
 hormones, 51-53
Femisexuals, 9
Fistulas, 73
Fragile X Syndrome, 35
Free University Hospital, 196
Frontal cranial reduction, 59

Garber, Marjorie, 7
Garland, Jack Bee, 7
Gay gene, 30-31
Gay pride march, 115
Gender, xxii
Gender Centre, Australia,
 76, 179
Gender dysphoria, xix, 170, 198
Gender Trust UK, 177, 197
Gendy's conference, 180-182
General Adaptation theory, 28
Genetics, 29-32
Goodfellow, Peter N., 36
Gooren, Professor Louis, 24-25,
 49, 182
Grant, Julia, 92-93
Green, Professor Richard, 99

Hage, J. Joris, 67, 69
Hamer, Dean, 30-31
Hermaphrodite, xx
 pseudo, xx
Hijra, 118
HIV infection,
 transsexuality and, 76
Homosexuality,
 *See Transsexuality, Homosexuality
 and Transgenderism*

Hormonal imbalances, 26
Hormonal treatment, 48-51
Hormones,
 in the womb, 27
 femisexuality and, 51-53
 mascusexuality and, 53-55
Human Genome Project, 30
Hypnotherapy, 80-83

Insurance, 106-107
International Conference on
 Transgendered Law &
 Employment Policy, 126, 176
 See also Randolph-Frye, Phyllis
Intersex groups, xx
Jaw lines, 58
Jones, Lynne, MP, 109
Jorgensen, Christine, 91

Klene, Petra, 94
Klinefelter's Syndrome, 35
Kirk, Dr. Sheila, 50, 195
Kushra, 118

Labia and clitoplasty, 70
Laser tattoo removal, 65
Laser treatment, 65
Law, the,
 See Politics and the Law
 children and the, 107-108
La-Zarus Training, 77
Lear, Amanda, 92
Lengthening of lower limbs, 58
Lesbians and transsexuals,
 123-124
Life test, 41-42
Liposuction, 64
Living as a transsexual, 91
Lovell-Badge, Robin, 36

Marriage, 110
Mastectomy, 65-66
Mascusexuality and hormones,
 53-55
Mascusexual, xxi

Mascusexuals, 6
in the old Czechoslovakia, 16
Medical profession, 106
Mermaids, 95, 177
Metaidoioplasty, 69
Mind manipulation, 79
Misdiagnosis, 39-40
Money, John, 125
Montgomery, Don, 79
Morse, Oliver, 49

Narcissistic factor, 46
New Zealand, 107, 111
Nichols, Les, 54-55
Neuro-Linguistic Programming,
19, 90

O'Keefe, Tracie, 196, 197
story, xxiii
paper by, 198-202
Orchidectomy, 51, 70
Pansexual, xxi
theory, 1
chart, 5
Penfield, Dr. Wilder, 81
PETA (People for the Ethical
Treatment of Animals), 55
Peterson, Maxine, 101
Phalloplasty, 66-69
Politics and the law, 103
Portugal, 107
Possible causes of transsexualism,
12-33
Prefemisexual, xxi
Premascusexual, xxi
Press for Change, 109, 126, 177
Primary
femisexual, xxii
mascusexual, xxii
transsexual, xxii, 87
Prison, transsexuals in, 101-102
Private members bill(UK) for the
rights of transsexuals, 109-110
Prolapse, 74

Prostitution and transsexuality,
100-101
Pseudo-hermaphrodite, xx
Psychiatry, 37-39
Psychosexual genetics, xxii, 170
Psychotherapeutic hypnosis, 82
Public transsexuals, 91-93
Purnell, Alice, 181, 183
P v S, 112

Randell, Dr. John, 37
Randolph-Frye, Phyllis, 114
*See also International Conference
on Transgendered Law and
Employment Policy*
Raymond, Janice, 121-123
See also The Transsexual Empire
Rees, Mark, 7, 92
Reid, Dr. Russell, 125
Re-incarnation, 25
Rejection factor, 42-44
Relationships, 97-98
Religion, 116-119
Rhinoplasty, 57-58
Rib removal, 60
Robertson, Bill, 76
Robinson, Stephenie, 77
Rossi, Ernest Lawrence, 32
Rutherford, Erica, 10

Schizophrenia, 17
Schützer, Marjorie Anne
Napewaśtewiñ, 149
Scrotoplasty, 69
Secondary
femisexual, xxii, 43
mascusexual, xxii
transsexual, xxii, 38, 88
Sex change, xix, 199
Sex reversed
female, 34-35
male, 34-35
Silicone
free floating, 61

Index

Social networks, importance of, 93-94
Spain, 107
Spain, Daphne, 112
SRY-gene, 36-37
Stereotypes, 12
Surgery, 55-57
    tracheal shave, 59
    for raising the vocal pitch, 59
    See contents for individual operations or under their separate headings in the index
Sweden, 107

Tamils, 117-118
The Transsexual Empire, 121
Third sex, the, 17
Tipton, Billy, 7
Toilets, 106
Tracheal shave surgery, 59
Transbisexual, xxii
Transgenderism, 114-116
Transgenderist, xx, 172-173
Transheterosexual, xxi
Transhomosexual, xxi
Translesbian, xxii, 115
Transmen, 200
Transsexual, xix
Transsexualism, xiv
    possible causes of, 12-33
    the current medical viewpoint, 125
    and feminism, 119-123

Transsexuality
    and prostitution, 100-101
    homosexuality and transgenderism, 114-116
    and HIV infection, 76
Transsexuals
    in prison, 101-102
    private members bill for the rights of, 109
    lesbians and, 123-124
Transvestite, xx, 38-39
Transwomen, 200
Treatment, hormonal, 48-51
Treatments, other, 77-83
Tula, 91
    See also Caroline Cossey
Turkey, 107
Turner's Syndrome, 35

Urethroplasty, 70

Vaginoplasty
Vatican, the, 117
Vocal pitch, surgery for raising the, 59
Voice training, 77

Whittle, Stephen, 111, 181
Wildeblood, Peter, 103
Winyanktehca, 118, 150
Work, a right to, 111

Xanith, 118

TRANS-✖-U-ALL
The Naked Difference
BY TRACIE O'KEEFE and KATRINA FOX

Please send me _____ copies of the above book, which is a comprehensive overview of the transsexual experience. I attach payment totalling _____ Cheques made payable to **EXTRAORDINARY PEOPLE PRESS,** which includes postage and packing. **My mailing address is:**

NAME _____

Address_____

Town _____ Zip/Post code _____

Country_____

If you are paying by credit card please fill in the following details:

Name of card holder _____ Card no _____

Statement address _____

Town_____ Zip/Post code _____ Country_____

Date of card issue _____ Date of expiry _____

SIGNATURE _____

Only VISA/DELTA/ACCESS/MASTERCARD/SWITCH CARDS ARE ACCEPTED. Please allow 28 days for delivery. Mail to EXTRAORDINARY PEOPLE PRESS, SUITE 412 TRIUMPH HOUSE, 185-191 REGENT ST., LONDON W1R 7WB, ENGLAND. Prices: UK £13.99/ Europe £14.99/USA&overseas £16.99. Payment can be made by cash in £Sterling or $US and £Sterling only by UK Cheque, Eurocheque, UK Postal Order, IMO, Credit cards. **This form can be faxed to 0171 439 3536 for credit card orders only.**
Info at http://easyweb.easynet.co.uk/~katfox/